The Bible brought John Bergsma to [...] tells that story well. But the greatest beauty of this book is in the love John found in the Catholic Church. This is an experience I share. God's love overflows here — in Jesus and Mary, in the saints and sacraments, in the devotional customs and rich traditions. It's so much more than we knew before. It's so much more than we could have imagined. My hope is that many non-Catholics will read this and come home — and many Catholics will read it and come to a deeper appreciation of all they have.

— *Scott Hahn, Chair of Biblical Theology and the*
New Evangelization at Franciscan University
of Steubenville, author, speaker

Dr. Bergsma doesn't simply tell us the story of his journey from Calvinism to Catholicism. He allows us to learn along with his "former" self how Scripture can lead an intellectually honest Christian to the fullness of the Catholic Faith, especially when studied alongside the early Church Fathers. This book is both fascinating and enlightening, not to mention a joy to read! I encourage anyone — but especially our non-Catholic brothers and sisters — to delve into this book with an open mind and heart. You might just find yourself stunned, as well!

— *Anna Mitchell, host/producer of*
the Son Rise Morning Show

I've been waiting for a book like this — honest yet loving, challenging yet sincere, truthful yet unitive — one that I could hand to my own Evangelical friends who are longing for "more" in their churches and faith journeys. Bergsma is a great Biblical teacher because he is, first and foremost, a true, Biblical disciple. This is a work that both Evangelicals and Catholics need to read and to share, often. This little gem is the kind of book that can foster the unity that Saint Paul wrote about and our Lord desires for His children.

— *Mark Hart, Executive Vice President, Life Teen*
International, author, speaker, SiriusXM radio host

STUNNED
BY
SCRIPTURE

How the Bible
Made Me Catholic

Dr. John S. Bergsma, Ph.D.

**Our
Sunday
Visitor**

www.osv.com
Our Sunday Visitor Publishing Division
Our Sunday Visitor, Inc.
Huntington, Indiana 46750

Our Sunday Visitor Publishing Division, Our Sunday Visitor, Inc., 200 Noll Plaza, Huntington, IN 46750; 1-800-348-2440.
ISBN: 978-1-61278-393-2 (Inventory No. T1760)
RELIGION/Christianity/Catholic
RELIGION/Christian Life/Spiritual Growth
RELIGION/Biblical Studies/Bible Study Guide

eISBN: 978-1-61278-397-0
LCCN: 2017960771

Cover design: Amanda Falk
Cover art: Shutterstock

PRINTED IN THE UNITED STATES OF AMERICA

About the Author

Dr. John Bergsma is Professor of Theology at the Franciscan University of Steubenville. He served as a Protestant pastor for four years before entering the Catholic Church in 2001 while pursuing a Ph.D. from the University of Notre Dame specializing in the Old Testament and the Dead Sea Scrolls. Since 2004, his primary work has been teaching Scripture to the theology and catechetics majors of Franciscan University of Steubenville. A frequent guest on Relevant Radio's *Drew Mariani Show* and Sacred Heart Radio's *Son Rise Morning Show*, Dr. Bergsma has appeared on EWTN's *The Journey Home* and *Life on the Rock*, and he speaks regularly at conferences and parishes nationwide. Dr. Bergsma has numerous academic and popular publications, including the books *Bible Basics for Catholics* and *New Testament Basics for Catholics* from Ave Maria Press. He and his wife, Dawn, reside with their eight children in Steubenville, Ohio.

CONTENTS

A Book I Never Would Have Written

This is a book I never thought I'd write. In fact, twenty years ago I would have been horrified if you'd told me I would write it one day.

It's a book about my journey into the Catholic Church and how Scripture played a major role in that process.

Twenty years ago, I was convinced that the Catholic Church was largely a false church that ignored — and was ignorant of — Scripture. I considered Catholics as targets for evangelization: they thought they could earn their way to heaven, and I had a responsibility to share with them the true Gospel — that salvation is a pure gift from God, received by faith alone.

But I'm getting ahead of myself. It might be best to return, calmly, to the beginning and sketch out a bit of my life's spiritual journey.

I was born in 1971, the last of five siblings by a gap of about six years. My father was a U.S. Navy chaplain. In the U.S. military, chaplains have to be sponsored by a denomination. My father was sponsored by a Dutch Calvinist denomination to which our family had belonged for at least three generations. Dutch Calvinists usually call their churches "Reformed."

Not many people have heard of Dutch Calvinism, but most people have heard of Presbyterians. Presbyterians are also Calvinists, but they originated in Scotland and England. Dutch Calvinists, then, are like Presbyterians, only they came from Holland. So, imagine Presbyterians with wooden shoes and windmill cookies, and you have a pretty good picture of the faith-culture of my extended family.

During my childhood, my father was transferred many times, as is typical of the Navy. I grew up in Hawaii, New Jersey, Virginia, Connecticut, California, and then back to Hawaii for high school. In high school, I was powerfully influenced by the youth pastor of the little Baptist church we attended near the Marine base where my father served. He took me aside, along with two other high school boys, and began to work with us in a relationship of personal discipleship. That fundamentally changed my understanding of the Christian faith and what it meant to be a disciple of Jesus. I have ever afterward remained convinced that personal discipleship is the only way to lasting growth and flourishing for individual Christians and the Church as a whole.

At the end of my high school years, I chose to apply to college. That involved narrowing my career possibilities. Since I had done well in a wide range of academic subjects, there were a number of career paths open to me, from highly technical fields to performing arts. I prayed to God: "I don't know what to choose. I feel like I could do anything!" I felt an inaudible answer come back from God: "If you think you can do anything, why not do what you are avoiding?"

What I had been avoiding was pastoral ministry. I had long felt a tug to follow my father's footsteps and become a preacher myself, if not a military chaplain. However, I didn't consider myself a people-person, and many things about the pastoral vocation scared me. As a result, I had put the idea far on the back burner.

When God's voice in my heart pulled it back to the front and center, my college choices suddenly became radically simplified. I tossed out all the college applications to secular schools and just mailed in the one to our denominational college, which was the only path to becoming a preacher in the church my family belonged to.

In the fall of 1989, I entered as a pre-seminary student at that school and finished in three years with a bachelor's degree in Classical Languages (Greek and Latin). I was required to study Greek in order to read the New Testament in the original language, and I decided to pick up Latin along the way. In the process, I also met my future wife, Dawn, and we married in 1993, after I had completed one year of seminary.

After a year or so, we found ourselves pregnant with our first son, and Dawn quit work to care for herself and the baby.

That left it to me to provide for the family *and* go to school for the rest of my seminary career. With a degree in Classical Languages, my best chances of employment were probably in food service! However, I did have a license from the denomination to lead worship services, and it just so happened that the tiny inner-city church we attended had just lost its pastor. Unable to afford a fully ordained minister, the church asked me to become the acting pastor, and I accepted at the amazing remuneration rate of $800 per month. Unbelievably, Dawn and I could afford to live on that in those days! Thus began the four-year stretch of urban ministry that was probably the most transformative experience of my life.

As the acting pastor of an impoverished inner-city Dutch Calvinist church with a mixed congregation of Caucasians, Hispanics, and African-Americans, the challenges were unrelenting and often excruciating. At the same time, I encountered the reality of God in a direct and experiential way, more profoundly than anything previous in my experience. In so many ways that I did not realize at the time, God was using these four years of urban ministry to prepare me to enter into the Catholic Church. How could four years of ministry as a Protestant pastor drive one toward the Catholic Church? Oh, let me count the ways!

Suffice it to say that after four years of inner-city ministry, I was really no longer a classic Protestant on the inside. I was very uncomfortable with certain Protestant theological tendencies, although I never would have described it like that. I didn't realize at the time that my issue was with Protestantism *per se*; I just felt like I was somehow in the wrong form of Protestantism and needed to find a church that "had it all together doctrinally."

In any event, by this time I had reached the end of my seminary career, and it was time to graduate, be ordained, and begin a lifelong career for my denomination. The problem was that my theological confusion was causing me to be very hesitant about making a long-term commitment to my denomination. At the same time, I couldn't continue as a part-time pastor at the small church I was serving, and I had no other job prospects. Plus, my family was growing with the recent addition of a third child.

It's pretty depressing to complete an eight-year program of schooling and then, at the end, find that you are not ready to step over the threshold and commit to the career you had worked so hard for. In fact, I got more than a little depressed, confused, and directionless. Being close to despair, I did something rash that many do when experiencing an emotional and psychological crisis: I applied to graduate school. I figured that another four years or so of schooling might buy me the time to straighten out my mind. So, I sent out applications to about a dozen schools that offered doctoral programs in Old Testament. The one that responded most enthusiastically was the University of Notre Dame.

It's a providential story how I even applied to that University in the first place. Essentially, I missed an exit off the freeway while returning from a weekend "mission" to Chicago with my teen youth group. I got off at another exit to turn around and found myself almost on the campus of Notre Dame (Exit 77 of the I-80/90 Indiana Toll Road). Surprised by this (I thought Notre Dame was in California), I decided to see if they offered a doctorate in Bible. Sure enough, a quick internet search a few days later revealed that they did, so I applied. South Bend, Indiana, offered an extremely low cost of living, and Notre Dame offered an extremely generous fellowship with stipend — so, with then-four kids and a wife to support, it was a no-brainer to accept Notre Dame's offer and move my family two hours south to the Hoosier state.

As providence would have it, one of the first persons I met at Notre Dame was Michael, a fellow graduate student in theology who had three qualities I never thought I'd find in one person: he was highly intelligent, filled with the Holy Spirit, and Catholic. Now, I'd met highly intelligent Catholics before, but they showed no presence of the Spirit in their lives and seemed to practice their faith — if at all — only to keep up appearances for their mothers, or something similar. I'd met highly-intelligent, Spirit-filled persons, but they were all Protestants. I'd met Spirit-filled Catholics before, but they all seemed like they were playing with fifty-one cards, and their elevator didn't reach the top floor.

But now there was this man in front of me whose Catholicism could not be dismissed as either a lack of devotion or a lack of intelligence. How could anyone with such evident love for Christ and extensive knowledge of theology remain in the Catholic Church? To say I was intrigued would be an understatement. I was *fascinated*, like someone sighting a UFO in broad daylight — or Moses staring at the burning bush, unable to understand how it was not consumed.

I arranged to meet with Michael one day a week to talk theology over lunch. I really wanted to get to understand what made him tick and how he could have any kind of coherent worldview given what seemed to me, at least, his opposing commitments to Christ and to the Catholic Church. In particular, I wanted to know how he would respond to all my apologetic arguments against the Catholic Church, the ones I had used to good effect when evangelizing Catholics in the inner city. To my surprise, Michael responded to my apologetic attacks on the Catholic Church by citing *Scripture*. In fact, he carried a small Bible with him, and he knew how to use it. When we got into disagreements about doctrine, there were several occasions where Michael could show that the plain sense of Scripture better supported Catholicism!

How ironic, I thought. Taking Scripture in its plain, literal sense was a major emphasis of Protestantism. Against the Catholic Church, we prided ourselves in direct obedience to the plain sense of Scripture. Yet when it came to central matters of disagreement — like the Eucharist — I found myself trying to *get around* the plain meaning of the Bible, whereas the Catholic Church was defending it! This was shocking to me. I was outside the Catholic Church largely because of the Bible, but there were crucial instances in which the Catholic Church took the Bible *more seriously than I did.* Among those instances, the Eucharist loomed very large.

Michael and I continued to have conversations about points of contention between Catholics and Protestants. However, after some time we reached a kind of stalemate, of the same sort as I used to run into with fellow Protestant clergy. He had his proof-texts; I had mine. I could see his case; he could see mine. But there was no one to arbitrate. At this point in our relationship Michael suggested that we start looking together at the Church Fathers, who might serve as an arbitrator between us. That sounded reasonable to me — but, as you'll see, it didn't turn out as I expected. The Fathers shocked me with their early and strong affirmation of the Real Presence of Christ in the Eucharist, based on the plain sense of Scripture! It began to dawn on me that if the Catholic claim that the Eucharist really was the Body of Christ was true, then that *was* a *big deal*. I began to think that, if the Eucharist really was the Body of Christ, I had to be where Christ's Body was — and it wasn't in any Protestant group. The implications scared me. In that moment, I saw I had to become Catholic to be with Jesus' Body — but that would involve a huge cultural shift away from my nuclear and extended family and all that I was comfortable with into a much larger, amazingly diverse religious culture that was foreign and even distasteful to me.

I hadn't yet solved in my head the issues with the papacy and with Mary. I wasn't sure, in fact, that I would ever be able to reconcile myself to those doctrines. Nonetheless, I reasoned like this: At the present moment, I was putting up with many doctrines and practices in my own denomination with which I did not agree, and yet I did not have the Body of Christ in the Eucharist. In the Catholic Church, I might likewise have to put up with many doctrines and practices with which I did not agree, but I *would* have the Body of Christ in the Eucharist. Advantage: Catholics.

So, without fully resolving the problems I had with the papacy and Mary, I decided, then and there in my basement apartment on the campus of the University of Notre Dame in the fall of 1999, that I was going to have to enter the Catholic Church. Of course, there was a lot more that had to be worked out. I needed to talk to my wife. I had to tell my family. We had to make practical and financial arrangements. All of that took some time, and I will talk about some of the issues that came up in the remainder of this book. But finally, on February 24, 2001, on the Saturday Vigil before Ash Wednesday, my wife Dawn and I were confirmed and received into the Catholic Church at St. Matthew's Co-Cathedral in South Bend, Indiana.

People often ask me: but how did you deal with this or that certain doctrine? How did you ever come to accept this or that

Catholic practice? That is the point of this book. I want to delve into many of these different areas and explain the many lines of thought through Scripture that kept leading me back to the Catholic Church. "All roads lead to Rome," they used to say. Indeed, what I found out during the several months I was debating with Michael was that all the interpretive "roads" through Scripture kept coming back to the Roman Catholic Church. I know that may sound strange, but I will try to explain how I was stunned by Scripture, and why and how the Bible provides reasons to be (or become) Catholic!

CHAPTER ONE

"John, *I* Am Your Father!"

The Bible and the Papacy

Men of my generation almost all have at least one cinematic experience burned into their memory: sitting in the theater watching a one-handed Luke Skywalker, clinging desperately to the sky bridge, stare in horror while Darth Vader announces: "Luke, *I* am your father!"

"No, no! It's impossible!" Luke moans, "Noooooooooo!"

This scene captures the emotions many converts to the Catholic Church have experienced. They discover that the Pope, the man they once viewed as the Antichrist, is actually their spiritual father. To their non-Catholic friends, they seem like they have gone over to the "dark side." Accepting the papacy is so synonymous with becoming Catholic, that many Protestants refer to conversion to Catholicism as "poping" ("Pope-ing"), as in, "Did you hear about John? He poped!"

After all, if there is one thing Protestants don't like about the Catholic Church, it is the papacy. In fact, Lutheran theologian Stephen Long argues that it is *the only thing* all Protestants hold against the Catholic Church.[1] After all, Protestantism is very diverse. Some Protestant group can probably be found that agrees with the Catholic Church on almost every doctrine — whether the Real Presence, or justification, or Apostolic Succession — but *none agree about the papacy*. Necessarily so: to come to agree with the Catholic Church about the papacy would require one to reconcile with the Pope and thus join the Catholic Church!

---

1 D. Stephen Long, "In Need of a Pope? Protestants and the Papacy," *The Christian Century*, May 17, 2005, https://www.christiancentury.org/article/2005-05/need-pope.

The papacy in one sense was not a big problem to me as a convert, and in another sense, it was. I mean this: I got over my bigotry that the Pope was the antichrist in my teen years (John Paul II helped many Protestants get past this bias). By the time I was in Protestant ministry, I had a generally positive view of the Pope. By the time I started to seriously consider Catholicism, I could even see the practical need for the Pope as a universal pastor of all Christians. The practical side of the papacy was not a problem. It was *papal infallibility* that took me a long time to accept.

It was only a few weeks into my conversations with Michael in the fall of 1999 that the topic of the papacy came up, and Michael (as I recall) made the point that, if we were serious about the unity of the worldwide Church, we needed one worldwide pastor. I immediately saw the validity of his point, based on my experiences in urban ministry.

During my four years of urban ministry in Michigan, I served a racially diverse neighborhood in the heart of the city together with my co-pastor, a remarkable man, a former heroin addict who had experienced a radical conversion, supernatural deliverance from addiction, and had been gifted with extraordinary graces in his walk with Christ. He was an African-American who had moved from Selma, Alabama, to Michigan as an adult. For four years, he was my closest friend and partner, and he eventually baptized three of my children.

My partner was popularly known in the neighborhood and in the church as "Brother William."[2] Both he and I were in courses of study for ordination within our denomination, although on different tracks. As God's providence would have it, Brother William finished his ordination track before I finished mine, and that created a problem for us. Up to this time, I had been the head pastor of our little urban mission because I was credentialed as a "licentiate," somewhat equivalent to a transitional deacon. But upon receiving ordination, Brother William would now "outrank" me in the ecclesiastical system, and so that forced the question on us: who would now take the lead?

---

2 Not his real name.

We briefly discussed a "dual pastoral" model in which neither of us was the ultimate authority. We briefly discussed it, but then quickly rejected it. Why? We knew it wouldn't work. Although it had been tried in various congregations we knew, neither of us knew of a single example where such a model was ultimately successful. What was the problem? Lack of unified vision and responsibility. Different interested parties within the congregation would play the two pastors off against each other, and — lacking one clear leader or authority — either the congregation would split or one of the pastors would leave.

Brother William summarized it in his characteristic Southern diction: "Can't be but *one* pastor in the Church!" — driving home the point that, for the sake of unity, there had to be a central leader with whom "the buck stopped."

I agreed (and still do). So, when Brother William was ordained, he "leapfrogged" me into the position of senior pastor. I took on the supporting role. It was necessary for the unity of our little church of seventy members or so. How much more so for a Church with over a billion members! There has to be a universal pastor if we are serious about the unity of the church.

During my years of pastoral ministry, I was involved in many ecumenical initiatives that sought to build church unity, including the Promise Keepers men's movement that attempted to bridge denominational boundaries among Christian men in America. I have been to many meetings and conventions where we talked, sang, and prayed for Christian unity. However, I never felt like anyone was serious about it. It was well and good to have ecumenical prayer meetings, but I knew when push came to shove, you would have to pry everyone's denominational distinctions out of their cold, dead fingers. If we had been really serious about unity, we would have had to submit our doctrinal differences to a common person or group of persons (a synod or council), and then abide by whatever decision resulted. I knew no one was ever going to do that: not the Calvinists, not the Baptists, not the Lutherans, not the Pentecostals, and so on. We were all convinced of the truth of our own positions. We were all paying lip service to unity, but for real unity to come about, there would have to be (among other things) a universal pastor with whom "the buck stopped."

So, years later, it didn't take long for my Catholic friend Michael to convince me of the *practical* need for a Pope. Since I was already favorably disposed, I was also pretty receptive to the biblical data when he laid it out. The key biblical passage for the papacy is found in Matthew 16, the famous dialogue between Jesus and Peter:

> Now when Jesus came into the district of Caesarea Philippi, he asked his disciples, "Who do men say that the Son of man is?" And they said, "Some say John the Baptist, others say Elijah, and others Jeremiah or one of the prophets." He said to them, "But who do you say that I am?" Simon Peter replied, "You are the Christ, the Son of the living God." And Jesus answered him, "Blessed are you, Simon Bar-jona! For flesh and blood has not revealed this to you, but my Father who is in heaven. And I tell you, you are Peter, and on this rock I will build my church, and the powers of death shall not prevail against it. I will give you the keys of the kingdom of heaven, and whatever you bind on earth shall be bound in heaven, and whatever you loose on earth shall be loosed in heaven." Then he strictly charged the disciples to tell no one that he was the Christ. (Matt 16:13–20)

In verse 18, Jesus gives Simon a new name, "Rock," which in the original language of the Gospel (Greek) is *petros*, from which we get the English name Peter. Reading in the original language, the point of verse 18 is clearer:

> "And I tell you, you are 'Rock,' and on this rock I will build my church."

Jesus was making Simon into a kind of human foundation stone for the community (the "Church," Greek *ekklesia*, Hebrew *qahal*) that he was establishing on earth.

Now, I knew from my seminary studies that John Calvin and many other Protestant theologians had bent over backwards to avoid the clear statement of the verse that Simon Peter was the human "foundation stone" on which Jesus would build his Church. It was popular to argue that the "rock" on which Jesus would build the Church was Peter's *confession of faith* in the previous verse, not Simon Peter himself. Sometimes, the difference in gender endings on the name "Peter" and the word "rock" were pointed out in order to prove that Simon Peter could not be the "rock" on which Jesus built his Church. The Greek reads:

> "And I tell you, you are *petros*, and on this *petra* I will build my Church."

There is a difference in ending between the two words. But this means nothing. It only marks the grammatical gender of the word. If you know a European language besides English, you know that nouns in most languages have an assigned gender that is marked by various endings or by the article used with the word. Often the assigned gender of a word makes no sense. For example, in German the word for "young woman" (*das Mädchen*) is in the *neuter* gender!

In Greek, the word for rock, *petra*, is grammatically feminine and takes the ending a, which is feminine. However, you can't make a feminine noun into a man's name. So, when *petra* is given as Simon's name, the ending is changed to the masculine -os, thus his name is *petros*. This is a little like adding the ending "-y" on the word "rock" to make the man's name "Rocky."

This is all simply a meaningless exercise of Greek grammar, and none of it would be relevant in Jesus' spoken language. The Gospels are written in Greek, which was the international language of the day, everyone's second language (like English in modern culture), in order to reach a large audience.

But Jesus usually spoke a different language, called Aramaic, with his disciples. We see a hint of untranslated Aramaic peeking through in Matthew 16, because the phrase "Bar-Jonah" in verse 17 is Aramaic for "son of John." So, Jesus was originally speaking in Aramaic when he made Peter the Rock of the Church, and in Aramaic the word for rock is *kepha*, and *kepha* cannot take any endings in Aramaic. The original spoken words of Jesus would have been:

> "And I tell you, you are *kepha* and on this *kepha* I will build my Church."

The word *kepha* was given a Greek masculine ending (-s) and appears nine times in our Bibles as "Cephas": John 1:42; 1 Corinthians 1:12, 3:22, 9:5, 15:5; Galations 1:18, 2:9, 11, 14.

The difference in gender of *petros* and *petra* is a grammatical issue that arose only when Jesus' original words were translated into Greek. Nonetheless, I had read convoluted apologetics that tried to make a big deal over it in order to separate Peter as a person from the "rock" on which Jesus would build the Church.

Yet even when I was a Protestant pastor and seminarian, I never bought Calvin's interpretation that the "rock" of the Church was Peter's *confession of faith* rather than Peter himself. That seemed so strained to me. It was so obvious that Jesus was changing Simon's name in order to signify the fact that he had become the rock of the Church. In my own mind, Calvin had just gone overboard trying to reject the position of the Catholic Church. Now that relations with the Catholic Church under John Paul II weren't so strained, I thought, we could all agree that Peter was the rock of the Church.

But to me, this meant no more than that Peter was the first Christian, and maybe had an important role in founding the Christian movement. It never occurred to me that this role of "rock" was a kind of office or position that would continue after Peter's death, with someone else taking on the role.

Here's where we need to turn to the next verse, verse 19:

> "I will give you the keys of the kingdom of heaven, and whatever you bind on earth shall be bound in heaven, and whatever you loose on earth shall be loosed in heaven."

I was told in the Protestant seminary that the "keys of the kingdom" were the preaching of the Gospel. When Peter preached the Gospel, those who accepted it would be "loosed in heaven" (saved) and those who rejected it would be "bound in heaven" (damned).

I accepted that view because I didn't know any better. I didn't know the Old Testament background for this verse. What I am about to show you was never shown to me in the seminary, and it rocked my world when I first saw it. Matthew 16:18–19 is actually drawing on a famous passage from the prophet Isaiah.

Thus says the Lord GOD of hosts, "Come, go to this steward, to Shebna, who is over the household, and say to him: What have you to do here and whom have you here, that you have hewn here a tomb for yourself, you who hew a tomb on the height, and carve a habitation for yourself in the rock?… I will thrust you from your office, and you will be cast down from your station. In that day I will call my servant Eliakim the son of Hilkiah, and I will clothe him with your robe, and will bind your girdle on him, and will commit your authority to his hand; and he shall be a father to the inhabitants of Jerusalem and to the house of Judah. And I will place on his shoulder the key of the house of David; he shall open, and none shall shut; and he shall shut, and none shall open." (Is 22:15–22)

Again, it amazes me that, even though we discussed Matthew 16:18–19 in several different classes in my seminary, no one ever pointed out the connection with the Isaiah passage, even though the connection is well-known among Bible scholars and mentioned in several commentaries. After all, there are only two places in the Old Testament where the word "key" is used (Judg 3:25; Isa 22:22), so when we look for the Old Testament background of Jesus' teaching (which we should always do), it doesn't take long to find the connection between Matthew 16:19 and Isaiah 22:22.

Be that as it may, let's discuss this passage of Isaiah and explain its relevance to Matthew 16:18–19.

The passage rebukes a certain man named Shebna. This Shebna was the royal steward, in Hebrew "the one over the house." In the ancient kingdom of David, the royal steward was second in power only to the king. He ran the king's household, and he had the keys to the palace. He controlled access to the king: he could lock or unlock the palace, let you in to see the king or keep you out.

Now, this particular royal steward, Shebna, had let his power go to his head. He began to think of himself as equal to the king, and was having a tomb carved for himself in the royal cemetery. If you are familiar with Tolkien's *Lord of the Rings*, think of the character of Denethor, steward of Gondor. Tolkien was something of a Bible scholar himself (he assisted in a Catholic translation of the Bible) and was well aware of the role of the royal steward. He modeled Denethor after Shebna. Both fell prey to pride and a desire to take the place of the king.

God sent Isaiah to Shebna with a message of rebuke. God would put Shebna out of office and replace him with a better man, Eliakim son of Hilkiah. Look what he says about Eliakim:

> "I will clothe him with your robe, and will bind your girdle on him, and will commit your authority to his hand; and he shall be a father to the inhabitants of Jerusalem and to the house of Judah."

Let's note two things. First, the "robe" and "girdle" were priestly garments because the royal steward was connected with the priesthood. It is highly probable that Eliakim was of priestly descent because his father's name, "Hilkiah," was popular within the Levitical priesthood.[3] Second, Eliakim will be a "father" to Jerusalem and the House of Judah. The "House of Judah" was a name for the entire kingdom of David. So, we see that the royal steward had a paternal or fatherly role for all the citizens of the kingdom. They looked to him as a father-figure: a provider and protector.

Do you see where this is going? The ancient kingdom of David had an important role for a second-in-command figure, a priestly character who was a "father" or "papa" to all the people in the kingdom. Sound familiar?

Before we bring home all the implications of that, let's proceed to the next verse:

> "And I will place on his shoulder the key of the house of David; he shall open, and none shall shut; and he shall shut, and none shall open."

Apparently, the key to the royal palace ("the key of the house of David") was worn on the shoulder of the royal steward as a sign

---

3 All the other Hilkiahs known in Scripture were priests.

or badge of his office. Perhaps it was tied there on his garment.[4] The statement "he shall open, and none shall shut" emphasizes the royal steward's authority no one but the king himself could oppose the steward's decisions.

Finally, let's notice the royal steward held a well-defined office or position that would be filled by another after he died or retired. So, God says to Shebna: "I will thrust you from your office (Hebrew *matsav*) and cast you down from your station (Hebrew *ma'amadh*)." It wasn't a charismatic role held by one person that disappeared with him, but the role continued perpetually.

With this background in mind, let's return to Matthew 16:19:

> "I will give you the keys of the kingdom of heaven, and whatever you bind on earth shall be bound in heaven, and whatever you loose on earth shall be loosed in heaven."

This statement is clearly modeled on the ancient prophecy of Isaiah, because we see the parallelism of the promise of the gift of the key followed by the promise of authority. The phrase "Whatever you bind on earth shall be bound in heaven" is strongly parallel to "He shall shut, and none shall open."

However, the *difference* between "binding and loosing" versus "shutting and opening" is just as instructive as the parallel.

In Jesus' day, the terms "binding and loosing" referred to the authoritative interpretation of divine law. In Jewish culture, this was (and is) called "halakhic" judgment. In Judaism, the *halakhah* refers to the way you put the Law of Moses into practice. It derives from *halakh*, the verb "to walk," and one could translate the term literally as "how one walks," or "how one behaves." Others have defined it as "the law as practiced."

We need to realize that the Law of Moses (and all law) requires interpretation. For example, the Law of Moses says to "rest" on the Sabbath day and refrain from "work."

---

4 See William Cooke Taylor, ed., *The Bible Cyclopaedia: Or, Illustrations of the Civil and Natural History of the Sacred Writings* (London: J.W. Parker, 1843), vol. 2, p. 718, where it is noted that the practice of wearing the key on the shoulder was still current among the Moors in the nineteenth century.

Now, let's say one is truly serious about obeying that command. Then several questions have to be answered: exactly when does the Sabbath begin, and when does it end, so I can be sure I'm not violating it? What constitutes "work" or "rest"? Is it "work" if I walk too far on the Sabbath? Is it "work" to light a fire? All these questions and hundreds more need to be answered if one is seriously going to obey the command to "rest."

All such questions are "halakhic" issues. As a matter of fact, the Jewish rabbis eventually decided that lighting a fire *was* work. Therefore, one could not cook or do any other activity requiring a fire to be lit on the Sabbath. Furthermore, any walk longer than about a kilometer from one's property became "work." So, Jewish communities tend to eat cold food on Saturday and build houses within a short distance from their synagogue.

The authority to make all these kinds of decisions about the interpretation of God's law was collectively termed "binding and loosing." To "bind" something was to forbid it; to "loose" something was to permit it. Lighting a fire was "bound" on the Sabbath, but walking a kilometer was "loosed."

So, when Jesus says to Peter, "*Whatever you bind on earth shall be bound in heaven, and whatever you loose on earth shall be loosed in heaven,*" he is conferring on Peter the authority to interpret divine law (i.e., Scripture), and promising him that *heaven will back up his judgments.*

Later in life, I was again shocked to discover how clearly Jewish scholars understand the profound authority that is being conferred on Peter in this passage. The *Jewish Encyclopedia* explains that the authority to "bind and loose" was not merely an academic or intellectual exercise, but a divinely given power. Prominent rabbis would "bind and loose" for ancient Jews, and it was not that the rabbis "merely decided what, according to the Law, was forbidden or allowed, but that they possessed and exercised the power of tying or untying a thing by the spell of their divine authority." The *Encyclopedia* continues:

> This power and authority ... received its ratification and final sanction from the celestial [heavenly] court of justice (Sifra, Emor, ix.; Mak. 23b). In this sense Jesus, when ap-

pointing his disciples to be his successors, used the familiar formula (Matt. xvi. 19, xviii. 18). By these words he virtually invested them with the same authority as that which he found belonging to the scribes and Pharisees.[5]

So, let's put this all together. Based on the background in Isaiah 22, we come to understand that bearing the "key of the kingdom" was the mark of office of the royal steward, the man over the palace and "number two" to the king himself. Therefore, Jesus' words to Peter in Matthew 16:18–19 confer on him the role of royal steward in his (Jesus') kingdom, and they also grant Peter the authority to make decisions about how to interpret divine law, particularly the Scriptures. In the Old Testament, the role of the royal steward was both priestly and paternal: it was filled by a man who wore priestly garments, and he was recognized as a "papa" by all the citizens of the kingdom. Moreover, this role was not a personal charism that died with the royal steward, but it was an "office" or "station" that was filled by another when the previous occupant died or was removed.

One has to be fairly blind not to see that this is model of the papacy!

During my journey into the Catholic Church, I began to realize this:

Jesus is both *Son of God* and *Son of David*; therefore, his kingdom is both *kingdom of God* and *kingdom of David*.

Once I realized that, *all sorts of things about the Bible and the Catholic Church began to make sense!*

Growing up, I never understood *why* the first two or three chapters of Matthew and Luke stressed so heavily Jesus' connection to the royal line of David, and yet the Davidic kingdom idea seems to go nowhere for the rest of the Gospels and the New Testament.

Actually, I was terribly mistaken. References to David and his kingdom actually continue through the Gospels and into Acts

---

5 See Kaufmann Kohler, "Binding and Loosing," *The Jewish Encyclopedia* (New York: Ktav, 1906), http://www.jewishencyclopedia.com/articles/3307-binding-and-loosing.

and occur elsewhere in the New Testament, especially in Revelation. The connection of Jesus to the fulfillment of the promises to the royal House of David is actually a major theme in the New Testament generally, but to grasp it we have to see that *the Church is the fulfillment of the kingdom of David.* That's why Jesus promises the Twelve that they will "sit on thrones judging the tribes of Israel" (Luke 22:30). When do they do that? When they rule authoritatively over the Church in Acts (see Acts 5:1–11, for example). The Church is the "Israel of God" (Gal 6:16).

The Catholic Church is the transformed kingdom of David. The Son of David, Christ the King, rules over it. On earth, the royal steward guides it, a priestly and paternal man, a man called "papa" or "pope" by the citizens of the kingdom. He can "bind and loose" by declaring what is in accord with divine law and what is prohibited by it. So, for example, when Paul VI judged in his encyclical *Humanae Vitae* that artificial contraceptives were prohibited by divine and natural law, it was an exercise of the power of "binding" given to Peter and his successors.

The doctrine of papal infallibility is already implied in Matthew 16:19 when we read it in light of Jewish religious culture and through Jewish eyes. We have already seen that the *Jewish Encyclopedia* understands "binding and loosing" as an exercise of divine authority, ratified and sanctioned by "the celestial court of justice." This is precisely what Jesus means by saying "what you bind on earth shall be bound in heaven." Heaven will confirm the decisions of Peter on earth; and surely this implies that heaven will first *guide* the decisions of Peter on earth, because heaven cannot confirm error. That implies infallibility.

However, I did not come to affirm papal infallibility merely for scriptural reasons, although I did see that Scripture implied it. Rather, I came to accept papal infallibility when I saw its relationship to Church unity.

Here is my line of logic. You can judge if I am faithful to Scripture in my thinking:

1. Jesus desires visible unity of his Church.
2. Visible unity requires, ultimately, one "senior pastor."

3. The job of the "senior pastor" is to maintain unity.
4. He can only maintain unity by stopping fights.
5. He can only stop fights if his word is final.
6. His word is final only if he can make an infallible judgment.

Did you follow that? Let me go through the steps with you, one by one.

1. Jesus desires visible unity of his Church.

Whether Catholic or Protestant, we Christians are not being honest with ourselves, church history, or the Scriptures if we deny this point.

I became convicted of the need for the visible unity of the Church when I had to prepare a sermon on John 17, the famous "High Priestly Prayer." In the part of this prayer where Jesus prays for the whole Church, he says:

> "I do not pray for these [i.e., the apostles] only, but also for those who believe in me through their word, that *they may all be one*; even as you, Father, are in me, and I in you, that they also may be in us, *so that the world may believe* that you have sent me." (John 17:20–21, emphasis added)

I knew that the usual Protestant interpretation of this passage was that Jesus was merely praying for spiritual unity, but my gut reaction to that, even as a Protestant, was "cop out!"

I could not believe — and still cannot believe — that Jesus was praying for his followers to be divided into forty thousand different groups differing on every imaginable point of doctrine, as long as they were somehow "spiritually unified" in some airy-fairy way.

I am especially convinced of this because it dawned on me — all those years ago when I was working on this text in the context of urban ministry — that there was a connection between *unity* and *mission*. Notice how the prayer that "they may all be one" is followed by the purpose clause "so that the world may believe." Therefore, the unity of the Church lends credibility to the Gospel and helps the world "to believe" that

Jesus has really been sent from God. But the world sees only the external. The world cannot see some airy-fairy "spiritual" unity behind forty thoudand or more bickering denominations. The world needs to see *visible* unity in order to be moved to belief. That's why the Reformation has *crippled* the evangelization of Western civilization, and it has been downhill for Christianity in the West ever since.

2. Visible unity requires, ultimately, one "senior pastor."

Almost all churches recognize this in practice. As I mentioned above, dual pastorships are occasionally tried, but they never work long term. This is especially true in the most successful churches, like mega-churches built around the personality of one senior pastor: Bill Hybels, Rick Warren, Joel Osteen. The buck has to stop with one man, otherwise the church will not stay moving in one direction. It will be split by different visions.

Why can we recognize this principle on the local level, but not apply it to the universal level?

I'll tell you why. Because, as I've said, most Christians *are not serious about Church unity.* They may pay lip service to ecumenical efforts, but they are not going to budge one inch on the theological particulars of their tradition in order to come back to a unified Church.

There's no problem with the logic: if the local church needs a pastor for unity, the universal church needs a pastor for unity. The problem is that folks don't like the conclusion.

Is there any indication that Jesus appointed one "senior pastor" over his Church? Absolutely! We just need to read the Scriptures with an open mind!

There is only one apostle whom Jesus names "the rock," says that he will build his "church" on, and gives the "keys of the kingdom," demonstrating that he has the role of the "royal steward" or second in command in the spiritual kingdom Jesus is establishing.

There is only one apostle who is *always* listed first in all the lists of apostles in the Gospel.

There is only one apostle who receives a triple commission to "feed and tend the sheep" in John 21, just before Jesus' ascension. Since the word "pastor" literally means "shepherd," and "senior" means "chief or primary," we can say quite literally that Jesus appointed Peter as the "senior pastor" on the shores of Galilee after his resurrection (John 21).

Folks may resist applying Peter's role to his successors, but the royal steward in the Old Testament had an "office and station" (Isa 22:19), and the replacement of Judas by Matthias in Acts 1 also demonstrates that the apostles had an "office" and "station" (Acts 1:20). In fact, the word for Judas's apostolic "office" is literally *episkopen* in Greek, from which we get the word "episcopal" and ultimately even "bishop."[6]

Peter ended is life crucified in Rome. The Roman Christians recognized his disciple Linus as his replacement; Linus in turn was replaced by Anacletus; and so on down to Pope Francis today. Jesus did not provide a "royal steward" only for the first thirty years of the Church's existence.

3. The job of the "senior pastor" is to maintain unity.

Not his sole job, of course, but one of his most important responsibilities: certainly within a local church, and all the more so in the church universal. We see indications of Peter's responsibility for unity in the Scriptures: Jesus prays that Peter's faith will not fail, so that afterward he can "strengthen your brothers" (Luke 22:32), i.e., the other apostles. Strengthening them would certainly include keeping them together. At the first Church council described in Acts 15, it is Peter whose speech ends debate (Acts 15:7–11). Notice there is much debate before Peter speaks (15:7) and none afterward (15:12–29). As a result, the early Church did not split into "First Church of the Circumcision" and "First Church of the Gentiles." Peter's ministry kept the Church together.

---

6 "Bishop" is a corruption of the Greek *episkopos*, "overseer" or "supervisor," through the German *bischof*.

4. He can only maintain unity by stopping fights.

This is simply obvious. Infighting, especially over theological issues, is what destroys Church unity. Different leaders have different opinions on a "hot button" issue, and before you know it, you've got two different denominations.

The weakness of Protestantism is that it lacks any way to resolve different plausible interpretations of Scripture.

If Jesus really intended the Church to remain together — which he did, according to John 17 — then he must have left us with the means to do it. Obviously, good intentions and the Holy Spirit are not those means, because Protestants have both of those and do not maintain unity. Christians have testified since the earliest fathers that one of the most important means to unity is the bishop of Rome, the successor of Peter, who is the touchstone of unity.[7] Those who reject this testimony of the early Fathers have the responsibility to propose some other workable means of unity that Jesus left us.

As we saw above, the Scriptures themselves portray Peter in this role of settling theological fights. In Acts 15, his speech to the council of Jerusalem (vv. 7–12) settles the issue. When James, the leader of the "losing party," rises to concede the argument, he cites the judgment of Peter (15:14) even before he cites the witness of Scripture (15:15–16). I don't wish to argue from that fact that Peter's testimony outweighs Scripture. But Acts 15:7–12 does show the authority Peter exercised within the early Church: an authority to settle divisive issues.

---

7 For example, around A.D. 180, the early Church Father Irenaeus, pastor of the city of Lyons in France, wrote the following about the Church of Rome: "It is a matter of necessity that every Church should agree with this Church, on account of its preeminent authority." Then immediately he proceeded to list the succession of bishops of Rome (i.e., Popes) from Peter down to Eleutherius, who was still Pope in Irenaeus's day: "Eleutherius does now, in the twelfth place from the apostles, hold the inheritance of the episcopate. In this order, and by this succession, the ecclesiastical tradition from the apostles, and the preaching of the truth, have come down to us" (Irenaeus, *Against Heresies*, Book III, Chapter 3, Sections 2–3; http://www.newadvent.org/fathers/0103303.htm).

5. He can't stop fights unless his word is final.

If his word isn't final, other leaders will just argue with him, and continue arguing with each other, thereby destroying the unity of the Church.

6. His word isn't final unless he is infallible.

Here's where we finally come to the rub. Even Protestants who respect the role of the successor of Peter and see the need for a universal pastor still balk at the idea that his formal decision is backed by the Holy Spirit and cannot be wrong. But let us clearly understand: unless the Pope is backed up by infallibility, even when he would attempt to put an end to a fight *people would just say he himself was wrong.* The fight would just continue and the Church break apart.

Infallibility is really what is implied when Jesus gives to Peter *personally* an authority that he bestows on the rest of the apostles only *corporately* (as a group), namely, "what you bind on earth will be bound in heaven, what you loose on earth will be loosed in heaven" (Matt 16:19; cf. Matt 18:18). This, as Jewish scholars attest, is the promise of the backing of the divine court for the decisions that Peter makes concerning the interpretation of divine law. It entails that Peter's decision is *infallible*, which means "unable to err."[8]

Let us clarify that the Catholic Church has never held that the successor of Peter (or Peter himself!) was personally sinless, or that he never makes a wrong decision. Only a *formal decision on doctrine* is protected from error — in Jewish terms, a halakhic judgment. What constitutes a *formal decision*? The Church has standards for how that needs to be expressed.[9] The technical term is that the Pope speaks *ex cathedra*, "from the throne," which is not so much that he must physically sit on the throne of the bish-

---

8 Not "unable to fail," a common misconception among English-speakers.

9 See the discussion in the online *Catholic Encyclopedia* under "Infallibility": http://www.newadvent.org/cathen/07790a.htm#IIIB.

op of Rome in St. John Lateran,[10] but that he *self-consciously* and *clearly* intends to pass judgment on a disputed question on behalf of the whole Church.

So, we've explained the argument to the end. Let's just run through it one more time to make sure we have grasped it: The job of the "senior pastor" of the universal Church is to keep unity, which he cannot do unless he can stop fights, and he can't stop fights unless his decision is final, which implies he is *infallible* or "unable to err." That's it. That's what I saw during my conversion to Catholicism, and I still see it today.

The Catholic Church remains one body, in part because of the gift of the papacy, the successor of Peter. Protestants have left the Catholic Church. Orthodox are separated from Peter. Like all who become separated from the Catholic Church, they have both been unable to maintain unity within their own ranks. Nonetheless, the Catholic Church remains a *single body*. It is *not* characteristic of Catholics to enter into schism. Great moral and spiritual reformers within Catholicism, unlike those within Protestantism, do not start new churches and break bonds of communion. No one ever says of Catholics that they are "the split C's" the way they say of Presbyterians, the "split P's." There really is a very different lived experience in being Catholic versus being something else.

Summing Up the Scriptural Stunners

I first opened up to the papacy because I saw the practical need for it. In time, however, I came to realize how strong the evidence for the papacy was within the Scriptures. To sum it up:

1. Matthew 16:18–19 establishes Peter as the "royal steward" of Jesus' kingdom-Church, and promises him the infallible backing of heaven for his decisions about the interpretation of divine law. A succession in office is implied by the fact that the royal steward of the Davidic kingdom was an office-holder with successors.

---

10 It is actually the Basilica of St. John Lateran (not St. Peter's Basilica) that is the cathedral of Rome, the "official" church of the Bishop of Rome, the Pope.

2. John 21:15–19 gives Peter an unparalleled and incomparable triple commissioning as the unique shepherd or "pastor" of all Christ's sheep.
3. Acts 1:15–26 establishes the principle that the apostles occupied an "office" (*episkopen*) that could be filled by another after their death, thus establishing the principle of "succession."
4. Acts 5:1–11, the account of Ananias and Sapphira, demonstrates that lying to and "testing" Peter is tantamount to lying to and testing the Holy Spirit.
5. Acts 15:1–31 shows Peter exercising his role as chief shepherd or "senior pastor" by putting an end to debate that threatened to break apart the unity of the early Church by rendering an authoritative judgment about the issue under question.

Does the Bible lay out a whole theory of the papacy? No, because that wasn't why it was written. Does the Bible reflect the fact that Peter was the divinely-authorized leader of the Church? Yes. Does early Church tradition reflect the fact that this role fell to his successor upon his death? Absolutely. Let's close with the testimony of Saint Jerome, the first great Bible translator of Christianity, from a letter addressed to Pope Damasus I (c. A.D. 376):

> I think it is my duty to consult the chair of Peter, and to turn to a church whose faith has been praised by Paul (Rom 1:8). I appeal for spiritual food to the church whence I have received the garb of Christ.… Away with all that is overweening; let the state of Roman majesty withdraw. My words are spoken to the successor of the fisherman, to the disciple of the cross. As I follow no leader save Christ, so I communicate with none but your blessedness, that is, with the chair of Peter. For this, I know, is the rock on which the church is built![11]

---

11 *Letter 15.2.* See NPNF 2, 6:18. See also *Sancti Eusebii Hieronymi: Epistulae 1-LXX*, ed. Isodorus Hilberg, *Corpus Scriptorum Ecclesiasticorum Latinarum* (CSEL), vol. 54 (Vienna: F. Tempsky, 1910), 63–64.

May we, like Jerome, combine dedication to the study of Scripture with loyalty to the Bishop of Rome, the successor of Peter.

CHAPTER TWO

Mary, Mary, Quite Contrary

The Bible and the Blessed Mother

For myself, as for many Protestants, the role of Mary in the Christian life was *the* major sticking point in the process of my conversion.

One memorable episode comes to mind. In the Fall of 1999, we had just moved to the University of Notre Dame. I was warming to the Catholic faith and had just read a modern Catholic apologist who had made some good points in favor of Catholicism, so mentally I was toying with the idea of becoming Catholic. I came home from class to our small, on-campus, basement apartment in the married student housing, and Dawn was there with the kids to greet me. She told me about a conversation she had earlier that day with another grad student wife who was a Catholic. They had talked about teaching the faith to children, and the Catholic mom had given her some catechetical material she used with her own kids. I picked up one of the booklets and opened it up. It happened that the page I turned to showed Jesus on the cross with his heart on fire. The stream of fire went up to heaven before the Father. So far, so good. But there was a catch. There was also a stream of fire leading from Jesus' heart to the heart of Mary standing below him, next to the cross. The hearts of Mary and Jesus were united by this stream of fire, which joined and went up before God.

I didn't really understand what this was meant to represent, and I definitely was not accustomed to the romanticized, even mawkish artistic style that Catholic children's books traditionally use. I was completely "freaked out" by what looked to me to be a denial of the exclusive role of Jesus Christ as the mediator between mankind and God the Father: "there is one mediator between God and men, the man Jesus Christ" (1 Tim 2:5). It confirmed all my worst fears about Catholic Mary-olatry. I tossed the booklet down and ran into the other room. I gave myself an internal tongue-lashing. "What were you thinking? Get control of yourself! This Catholic stuff is crazy idolatry. You can't go down this path. You've got to stop reading those Catholic apologists!"

But the attraction was just too great. The beauty was too much to resist. My resolution only lasted about a week, and then I was back to reading Catholic literature and talking to my friend Michael about the Church again.

Sometime later, I was eating lunch with Michael and debating theology with him when I got frustrated by the fact that he seemed to have a response for every accusation I could hurl against the Catholic Church. It so happened that, looking around the venue where I was sitting, I could see an image of Mary presented as Queen of Heaven on the wall (such images, inspired by Our Lady of Guadalupe, are common on the campus, whether in sculpture, relief, painting, or another medium). "Look," I said to Michael, "where do you Catholics get this idea that Mary is Queen of Heaven? Isn't that title on the verge of blasphemy? I challenge you to point to *any scriptural evidence at all* that Mary is 'Queen of Heaven'!"

I sat back in my chair, a little self-satisfied that I had "pinned him to the wall" with the barbed shaft of a theological weapon. But Mike didn't seem taken aback at all. He was neither shocked nor impressed. Without missing a beat, he said, "What about Revelation 12?"

"What do you mean? What *about* Revelation 12?"

"You've read it, right?"

"Of course. I've read the whole book of Revelation at least three times. My mom started me reading the Bible through each year when I was twelve."

"Well, let's think about it. You know how it has a woman clothed with the sun and the moon under her feet, right?"

"Right."

"So she's in the heavens?"

"Yes."

"And she's got a crown of twelve stars, so she's a queen, right?"

"I suppose."

"And then she gives birth to a male child who's destined to rule the nations with a rod of iron. No doubt about who that is, right?"

"No, that's a reference to the messianic 'son of David' from Psalm 2."

"So we have a heavenly queen who gives birth to the Davidic Messiah. Couldn't that be a reference to Mary, the only woman in Scripture who gives birth to a Messiah?"

I just looked at him in silence, and then glanced away in a huff. "You're so clever I feel like you could prove to me this trash can over here is worthy of divine veneration," I said in frustration.

But inside, I was impressed. Later, when I had the opportunity, I looked at Revelation 12:1–5 again and thought about it. I had spent several years of my childhood in Baptist churches near the various military bases where we lived. There I was exposed to Baptist end-times teaching. It was often quite elaborate, with various current events linked to different verses of Revelation by an exegetical hair. Inevitably, they found ways to see the threat of Russian communism and other current affairs in the text.

I would ask my father about these interpretations, and he just told me to keep an open mind. "Maybe," he would say. "It's a possible way to read the text." Personally, he was unconvinced — as was I — but we allowed it *could* be true. So, I had always given the benefit of the doubt to my Baptist friends.

But now I was being confronted with a Catholic interpretation of Scripture that was relatively straightforward. The logic was not excessively contorted. It wasn't contorted at all: "We have a heavenly queen here who gives birth to Jesus; may it not be a reference, in some way, to the woman who actually gives birth to Jesus?" I had always given the benefit of the doubt to my Baptist friends with their proofs that the "beast from the sea" (13:1) was Russia or some similar view. Could I, in all honesty, deny the same benefit of the doubt to my Catholic friend? Could it be that there was some scriptural basis for Mary as "Queen of Heaven"? Could one plausibly interpret the Bible that way? If so, could there be scriptural support for other Catholic doctrines as well?

This was not the final moment of an intellectual conversion for me, but it was pivotal in my long journey toward the Catholic Church. Prior to this, when I heard Catholic arguments from Scripture, I simply shut down intellectually. I was convinced that there was no possible way the arguments were correct. Therefore, if they seemed to be correct, it was an illusion or sophistry, and I just had to figure out where the "trick" had been slipped in. However, after the discussion of Mary Queen of Heaven and Revelation 12, I began to actually open my mind to consider the merits of the arguments that were being made. My attitude shifted from, "None of this could possibly be correct," to, "Could there be some merit to this argument?"

I didn't feel then that I could rule out the possibility that the woman of this passage was, in some sense, Mary. But let's deal with the objections that some raise with the identification.

> And a great portent appeared in heaven, a woman clothed with the sun, with the moon under her feet, and on her head a crown of twelve stars; she was with child and she cried out in her pangs of birth, in anguish for delivery. And another portent appeared in heaven; behold, a great red dragon, with seven heads and ten horns, and seven diadems upon his heads. His tail swept down a third of the stars of heaven, and cast them to the earth. And the dragon stood before the woman who was about to bear a child, that he might devour her child when she brought it forth; she brought forth a male child, one who is to rule all the nations with a rod of iron, but her child was caught up to God and to his throne, and the woman fled into the wilderness, where she has a place prepared by God, in which to be nourished for one thousand two hundred and sixty days. (Rev 12:1–6)

Some say the woman of Revelation 12 can *only* be a personification of the Jewish people. Really? Why? Well, they say, she's wearing a crown of twelve stars, and that represents the twelve tribes of Israel. Indeed, I agree. However, wouldn't a crown of twelve stars be an appropriate headpiece for Israel's queen mother, herself a royal descendant of David? I think so. At most, the crown of twelve stars indicates the woman is Israel's queen.

Other details of the passage will not fit an identification of the woman as the Jewish nation. After the birth of the Messiah (12:5), the woman flees into the wilderness where she is protected by God. How would that apply to the Jewish people? It doesn't. Mary, however, fled to Egypt under the protection of Saint Joseph after the birth of Jesus. A similar flight to safety occurs in verse 14; again, this doesn't correspond to any event in the life of the Jewish people. Finally, verse 17 refers to the offspring of this woman as "those who bear testimony to Jesus." Did the author of Revelation really intend us to think that those who testify to Jesus are "offspring of the Jewish nation"? That's a bit of a stretch.

Let me state emphatically that it does *not* work to identify the woman of Revelation 12 as a symbol of the ethnic Jewish nation.

Others take her as a symbol of the Church. The biggest impediment to this view is that the text portrays the woman as pre-existing and giving birth to Christ; whereas it is more appropriate to think of Jesus Christ as pre-existing and giving birth to *the Church* in the blood and water from his side at the cross (John 19:34). It is true that, in a spiritual sense, the Church "gives birth to Christ" in the world every time she baptizes a new Christian; however, the birth of the "male child" in Revelation 12:5 is clearly not a description of the conversion of sinners, but of the historical birth of Christ and his subsequent ascension ("caught up to God and to his throne," v. 12:5).

Therefore, it does *not* work to consider the woman merely as a personification of the Church.

Others say, "She can't be an individual. She is a representative figure." Why is that?

The dragon that opposes her is not just a representative figure. He is an individual: the Devil or Satan (v. 12:9).

The child she bears is not just a representative figure, but Jesus the Christ, an individual.

Why can't she, too, be an individual?

I have come to believe that the woman of Revelation 12 is "Mary as icon of the people of God, Old Testament and New."

The crown of twelve stars does suggest her queenship over Israel, as well as the fact that she pre-exists Christ. But other details suggest the Church: the gift of wings and flight into the wilderness from the dragon in verses 13–14 suggest some escape of the early Christian community from destruction. Perhaps it refers to the flight of the Jewish "mother church" of Jerusalem to the town of Pella before the advancing Roman armies in the late A.D. 60s, as the early church historian Eusebius records. Perhaps the Blessed Mother was still with the Jerusalem church for this flight, although she would have been in her eighties by then. She would have been old, but it's not impossible, for Anna the prophetess was still active at that age (cf. Luke 2:37).

The attempt of the dragon to kill the Christ child upon his birth and the subsequent flight of the queen mother into the wilderness suggests a highly symbolic and theologized reflection of the events of Matthew 1–2: the birth of Jesus to Mary of the lineage of David, followed by Herod's attempt to kill the child and the flight into Egypt.

In any event, I don't see how anyone can *rule out* the possibility that the portrayal of a royal woman in Revelation 12 who gives birth to Jesus is, in some sense, a representation or allusion to Mary, the Queen Mother. For heaven's sake, much wilder and more speculative interpretations of Revelation have been proposed with great solemnity by preachers, scholars, and theologians throughout Church history!

Looking at Revelation 12 opened me to the possibility that there *was* some scriptural support for Catholic beliefs that had previously seemed insupportable.

Further, there were a series of clarifications that softened me to Catholic Marian doctrines and devotion.

First, my Catholic friends taught me the difference between *veneration* and *adoration*. They insisted that they *venerated* (honored) Mary and the other saints, but *adored* (worshiped) only God. This seemed to me to be a distinction without a difference at first, because the things they said and did in Marian devotion sure looked like *worship* to me. However, I was conditioned by Protestant piety. In Protestantism, we seldom knelt or bowed to anyone, not even to God. Our expressions of honor and worship were so tepid and bland, no wonder I thought Catholics worshiped Mary: what they did for Mary was more than I was used to doing for God!

However, when I saw what Catholics did in Eucharistic *adoration*, I realized there really was a distinction between their devotion to Christ and their devotion to Mary. The first time I visited a Eucharistic adoration chapel, for example, and saw Catholics *prostrate on the ground* in front of Jesus in the Blessed Sacrament, it made reciting the Rosary seem mild in comparison. There really are profound words and gestures that Catholics reserve for God alone.

Second, I got some clarity on what it meant to call Mary "Co-Redemptrix," or "Co-redeemer with Christ." At first, this sounded to me like Mary's role in the redemption of humanity was being placed on a completely equal footing as that of Christ. However, that's not the case. The Bible calls *every* Christian to be a co-redeemer with Christ, cooperating with Christ for the redemption of the world. We see this concept expressed in the following texts:

> [We are] fellow heirs with Christ, provided we suffer with him in order that we may also be glorified with him. (Rom 8:17)

Here Paul stresses how we are conformed or made like Christ, such that we "suffer with" him. Since Christ redeems through his sufferings, this "suffering with" amounts to co- (with) *redemption* (salvific suffering).

Saint Paul is even more emphatic elsewhere:

> Now I rejoice in my sufferings for your sake, and in my flesh I complete what is lacking in Christ's afflictions for the sake of his body, that is, the church. (Col 1:24)

Notice that Paul says his sufferings are "for your sake," which means they are *redemptive*: they have a purpose — they benefit the Colossians. They are not merely sufferings that result from sin or occur for some random reason. But Paul goes on: "I complete what is lacking in Christ's afflictions for the sake of his body the

Church." The same concept is at work. Paul's sufferings help the Church. They have a *redemptive* or *salvific* value. In some way, they are a participation in Christ's sufferings.

As a Protestant, I could never make sense of the phrase "what is lacking in Christ's afflictions" because I felt there could be nothing lacking in the afflictions Christ suffered for our redemption. But my friend Michael explained this passage in one sentence: "What could be lacking in Christ's afflictions except our participation in them?" Of course! That made sense within the context, because Paul is speaking precisely about sharing in the afflictions of Christ.

Mary was called — indeed, had a vocation — to share in Christ's suffering in a very singular and extraordinary way. The Scriptures make this clear. When she and Saint Joseph presented the infant Jesus in the Temple, Simeon said to her:

> "Behold, this child is set for the fall and rising
>   of many in Israel,
> and for a sign that is spoken against
> and a sword will pierce through your own soul also."
> (Luke 2:34–35)

That the sword will pierce through Mary's soul refers to intense interior suffering — is it not a frightening image for one's soul to be thrust through with a sword? The fact that this will occur to her "also" implies that it will occur to someone else as well. Simeon must have in mind the sufferings of Jesus. He already foreshadows Jesus' sufferings when he declares that the child will be a "sign that is spoken against," that is, criticized, opposed, and persecuted. Like her son, Mary will not escape this persecution, but "a sword will pierce through" her soul also.

Is there anyone else in Scripture to whom such a frightful prophecy of interior suffering is given? It happens to her "also," which means "with," so is this not a prophecy of co- (with) *suffering* with Jesus?

Likewise, we see Mary's co-suffering in Revelation 12. There, portrayed as the heavenly queen mother of Israel, she cries "out in her pangs of birth, in anguish for delivery." Surely this indicates the suffering of Mary to give Christ to the world. Does it just mean the regular physical pains of giving birth to a son? I highly doubt that typical physical birth pains would be so significant that they would be immortalized in this vision in Revelation 12. After all, most mothers undergo those, and they are quickly forgotten. No, the crying out in pangs and anguish must refer to a more profound suffering involved with bringing Christ into the world. I think we are justified in seeing it as a summary of all the co-suffering of Mary's life, all the anguish that being the Mother of the Messiah involved. Mary is also the icon and embodiment of the Church, which also suffers as a mother to give birth to Christ to the world.

Coming back to the idea of co-redemption: we have seen in Saint Paul that all Christians are called to participate in the sufferings of Christ for the redemption of the world. Thus, we are all called to a kind of *co-redemption* with a small "c." However, Mary's co-redemption deserves a capital "C," because it was of a very extraordinary nature. Her co-redemptive sufferings are immortalized in two dramatic places in the Bible (Luke 2:34; Rev 12:2). Yours and mine are not.

We all feel sorrow on Good Friday when we meditate on Christ's passion and the fact that our sins were the cause of it. But few of us can quite imagine what Mary experienced, since the one suffering on the cross was her own flesh and blood, the baby she gave birth to in Bethlehem.

I remember the first time I saw the word "co-redemption" used in Catholic spiritual writing to refer to the role of all of us Christians (it was in the writings of Saint Josemaría Escrivá). When I saw that, I said to myself, "Okay, they're not just making this up. They do have a spirituality of co-redemption for everyone, for the whole Church. Mary is 'Co-redemptrix' with a capital 'C' because her Christian vocation was unique and special. I can live with that."

So, the Scriptures that I mentioned above got me past my initial problems with Mary. I still found that some Catholic Marian practices were exaggerated. But I could understand why the Scriptures did offer some suggestion of a unique role for Mary.

I also noticed that the Catholics who had the greatest devotion for Mary also seemed to have the highest respect for

Scripture. Jesus told us, "You can tell them by their fruits" (Matt 7:16). I could not see how a bad devotion would lead someone to honor Scripture. So, although I didn't have all my t's crossed and i's dotted concerning Marian doctrines, I could accept Mary enough to become a Catholic.

Surprisingly, the whole "Mary" thing did not actually click with me fully until I had the responsibility of teaching Scripture at a Catholic university. I finished my doctorate in 2004 and was hired that same year to teach introductory classes in Old and New Testament at the Franciscan University of Steubenville, which has more theology majors (around 500 in the average graduating class) than any other Catholic university in North America.

About halfway through my first Fall semester, I had lectured my way from Genesis up through 2 Samuel. I was preparing my lecture on 1 Kings when I ran into this text:

> Then Adonijah … came to Bathsheba the mother of Solomon…. And he said, "Pray ask King Solomon — he will not refuse you — to give me Abishag the Shunammite as my wife." Bathsheba said, "Very well; I will speak for you to the king."
>
> So Bathsheba went to King Solomon, to speak to him on behalf of Adonijah. And the king rose to meet her, and bowed down to her; then he sat on his throne, and had a throne brought for the king's mother; and she sat on his right. Then she said, "I have one small request to make of you; do not refuse me." And the king said to her, "Make your request, my mother; for I will not refuse you." (1 Kings 2:13–20)

As I began to meditate on the backstory and the dynamic of what was going on here, I realized I had stumbled upon a very illuminating typology for understanding Marian doctrine.

The backstory here is that Solomon has just been made king in place of his father David. Before Solomon was enthroned, the heir apparent was his older brother, Adonijah. Adonijah had actually plotted his own inauguration as king, but called it off when his father, David, intervened and put Solomon on the throne immediately.

Now, Adonijah had not given up on his hopes of being king. He was, in fact, plotting a coup at this very moment. Abishag the Shunamite was a key pawn in the strategy of this coup. As distasteful as it sounds to us today, in ancient times a new king would often marry all the younger wives of the previous king. Possession of the royal women was a key sign and mark of political legitimacy. Abishag was recognized as King David's youngest and most recent wife. Adonijah hoped to acquire her, and thus increase his political capital to appear more legitimate than Solomon. Then, coordinating his supporters within the army, the priesthood, and the bureaucracy, he hoped to become king and put Solomon, his rival, to death.

However, Adonijah didn't want to risk asking Solomon directly for Abishag. So he attempted a work-around: he goes through the queen mother. In ancient Israel, kings often had several wives, and so it was the king's mother who reigned as queen. This is so different from modern culture, where the queen mother (for example, in England) plays a relatively insignificant role.

In antiquity, the queen mother was an extremely influential person in the kingdom. She had direct access to the king. Moreover, court protocol demanded that she receive whatever she requested from the king. If someone could gain an audience with the queen mother, she was often able to cut through all the "red tape" and intervene directly with the king in order to get something done.

That's the situation in 1 Kings 2:13–20. Adonijah approaches Bathsheba, the queen mother, to ask her to intercede for him before the king, confident that what she asks of the king will not be refused. See how each player in this drama presumes that the request of the queen will be granted:

> "Pray ask King Solomon — he will not refuse you."
>
> "I have one small request … do not refuse me."
>
> "Make your request, my mother, for I will not refuse you."

Apparently, that was court protocol. The queen mother got whatever she asked for in the presence of the king.

Also notice the dignity with which the king treats the queen mother:

> The king rose to greet her, and *bowed down to her.*

At this time in history, Solomon ruled one of the most powerful empires in the known world. To how many people do you think he bowed down? That's right. To nobody. Except his own mom. The queen mother was the only person in the kingdom whom *the king himself venerated.*

He also recognized her royal standing:

> He sat on his throne, and had a throne brought for the king's mother; and she sat on his right.

Some English translations read: "He sat on his throne, and had a seat brought for the king's mother." This is incorrect. The Hebrew word for Solomon's seat and his mother's seat is the same: *kisse'.* There's no reason to translate with two different English words. "He sat on this throne, and had a throne brought" for his mother. That's the meaning of the text. "She sat on his right." That was the position of dignity and authority. The one who sat on the right hand of the king was recognized as sharing the king's status or power.[1]

With all this in mind, imagine my experience when I first read over this passage to prepare a lecture on it for the eighteen- to twenty-two-year-olds who populated my Scripture courses. What does this passage mean for Christians today? What could I say about it? Well, obviously, Solomon is the Son of David, a well-known type of Christ. But Bathsheba, the mother of the king, of whom was she a type? Well … duh!

I had just stumbled onto perhaps the most important ty-pological passage in the Old Testament concerning the role of the mother of the king in the kingdom of David. The important thing here is not the political machinations of Adonijah. The important thing is what this passage reveals about the role and the status of the queen mother in the kingdom. Let's note three primary aspects of her role and status that it reveals:

---

1 See Ps 110:1; Matt 22:44, 26:64; Mark 16:19; Acts 2:33–34, 7:55–56.

1. Intercession. The queen mother served as an intercessor for those who, for whatever reason, could not get their request heard or granted directly by the king. She was, as it were, a court of last resort. If the typical channels for submitting a request to the king did not work, one could go to the queen mother and make one's appeal to her.

2. Veneration. The queen mother was so honored in the kingdom that even the king himself would bow down to her.

3. Coronation. The queen mother's status and dignity were recognized by symbolic acts; in this passage, by her *enthronement* at the right hand of the king. This was the ritual equivalent of receiving a crown (*coronation*), a scepter, or some other ceremonial act of investment with authority.

What's the meaning of this passage for us today? It typifies the roles that are now perfectly fulfilled by Mary, the queen mother in the transformed kingdom of David that we call the Church!

I had already come to understand that the Church was the beginning of the kingdom of God on earth. But the King of the kingdom of God was Jesus Christ, who was both Son of God and Son of David. That made it *necessarily* the case that the kingdom of God was also the kingdom of David. To deny that reality would be to deny the incarnation.

I had also already come to understand that Jesus restored certain structures of the kingdom of David already in his earthly ministry. The Davidic kingdom had a royal steward (Is 22:22), and Jesus appoints Peter to that role in Matthew 16:18. The Davidic kingdom had twelve officers over the "the house of Israel" (1 Kings 4:7–19), each one named. So, Jesus appoints twelve officers (Matt 10:1), each one named (Matt 10:2–4), and sends them out to the "house of Israel" (Matt 10:6), and later promises them "thrones" (Matt 19:28), just as the Davidic princes sat on thrones (Ps 122:5).

So, if Jesus restores the Davidic royal steward (Matt 16:18–19) and the Davidic twelve officers (Matt 10:1–6), it makes sense that he also restores the queen mother! What was her role? To *intercede* for members of the kingdom, especially members of the royal family, before the king; and whatever she asks for is granted! The words of the Memorare came back to me:

> Never was it known that anyone who fled to thy protection, implored thy help, or sought thy intercession was left unaided.

In recognition of this role, Mary receives honor or *veneration* from the members of the kingdom, and ceremonial recognition of her status (think of the last Glorious Mystery of the Rosary — the *Coronation*).

It was a real breakthrough for me to see this, because up to this point in time, I had accepted the Marian doctrines largely by trust in the Church's tradition and the fact that certain New Testament texts, such as Revelation 12, did seem to indicate some special status of the mother of the Messiah. But now I was beginning to see how the role of Mary in the Church was rooted in the Old Testament reality of the kingdom of David, which was restored by Christ and manifested visibly in the Church. The role of Mary as queen mother is not some "medieval add-on" to the faith of Christianity, but an organic development within salvation history.

Realizing the significance of 1 Kings 2 for what it reveals about the ancient role of the queen mother, I returned to the New Testament and asked the question, "Are there any texts in the second half of the canon that also reflect Mary's role as queen mother?"

Of course, there were. Revelation 12 comes to mind again, and we immediately recognize that this text reflects the traditions of the Davidic kingdom. The heavenly woman is portrayed as the queen mother of Israel, with the crown of twelve stars representing the twelve tribes. Being clothed with the sun and the moon under her feet probably reflects the great beauty of the perfect royal spouse in Song of Songs 8:10 ("fair as the moon, bright as the sun") and the brilliant golden robes of the queen in Psalm 45:9, 13.

But I also returned to the infancy narratives of Luke 1–2 and looked them over once more for signs of Mary's royal status. Suddenly, I found an explanation for a curious feature of the account of the Visitation in Luke 1:39–45. I had always found it a little odd that Elizabeth seems to fall all over herself welcoming Mary in verses 41–45, in a way that is all out of proportion to the culture of that time.

In graduate school, I was taught to read the biblical texts with a sensitivity to ancient culture and expectations. From that perspective, Mary and Elizabeth were two women of vastly different social standing. Mary was a teenager, perhaps around fifteen (a typical age of betrothal), espoused to a manual laborer from the hill country of Galilee — almost a "hillbilly" if you will. By contrast, Elizabeth was an elderly woman of high status. She lived near Jerusalem — the "New York" of its day, the cultural and economic capital of Judea — and her husband was a high-ranking priest (Luke 1:5) whose genealogy suited him to be a candidate for burning incense in the holy place, an honored duty (Luke 1:8–9). To help my students get the contrast, I often say it's as if Mary is the teenage fiancée of a construction worker from West Virginia, whereas Elizabeth is the wife of an important New York family who commutes to "the city" from their home in Connecticut.

In ancient societies, even more so than today, honor flows from younger to older, from low status to high status. When Mary shows up to visit Elizabeth in Luke 1:39, we would expect Mary to defer to Elizabeth, and pay her all sorts of respect. But that's the reverse of what we see! Let's read the famous passage again:

> In those days Mary arose and went with haste into the hill country, to a city of Judah, and she entered the house of Zechariah and greeted Elizabeth. And when Elizabeth heard the greeting of Mary, the babe leaped in her womb; and Elizabeth was filled with the Holy Spirit and she exclaimed with a loud cry, "Blessed are you among women, and blessed is the fruit of your womb! And why is this granted me, that the mother of my Lord should come to me? For behold, when the voice of your greeting came to my ears, the babe in my womb leaped for joy. And blessed is she who believed that there would be a fulfilment of

what was spoken to her from the Lord." And Mary said,
"My soul magnifies the Lord." (Luke 1:39–46)

Elizabeth's greeting of Mary is over the top. "Blessed are you among
women" is a Hebrew idiom that means "you are the *most blessed* of
all women." Hebrew and related languages lack superlative forms
("most," "greatest," "best") and have to use circumlocutions like
this phrase. I suspect that most English-speaking Christians are
unaware of the force of this verse in the original language: Mary
is the *uniquely blessed* woman in all human history.

But Elizabeth goes on: "Why is this granted to me, that the
mother of my Lord should come to me?" The phrase "why is this
granted to me" shows that Elizabeth regards it as a great *privilege*
that Mary should come to visit her home. Elizabeth regards it as
an *honor.* But why would this high-status lady in her wine, cheese,
and caviar world regard it as an *honor* for her pregnant teenaged
cousin from West Virginia to show up on the porch of her Connecticut estate?

The next phrase explains it: "That *the mother of my Lord*
should come to me." The "mother of my Lord" is a title for the
queen mother, the mother of the king. Elizabeth is falling all over
herself to welcome Mary because the Holy Spirit has given her
insight to recognize a truth that is not obvious to the rest of the
world: Mary is royalty, the greatest female royal of human history,
because she is queen mother of the Son of David who is destined
to "rule the nations with a rod of iron" (Ps 2:9; Rev 12:5).

In fact, Luke 1:39–45 is the first recorded act of *human
veneration* of the Blessed Virgin Mary. Understood within the
culture of the day, there is no doubt that Elizabeth is *venerating*
or *honoring* her younger cousin in a superlative fashion. If other
Christians want to challenge Catholics about the veneration of
Mary, the best response would be to say: "It's biblical! Mary is
already venerated in Scripture." Not only does Elizabeth venerate
her by calling her the most blessed woman and "mother of my
Lord," but Mary goes on herself to prophesy by the Holy Spirit
that she would be honored perpetually in the future: "henceforth
all generations will call me blessed."

I used to tell my students that the Visitation was the first recorded act of Marian veneration, but I had to modify that to "human veneration" after a student raised his hand one day and said, "What about the angel?" It's true: Gabriel already venerated Mary when he greeted her at the Annunciation.

Let's look again at Gabriel's greeting of Mary in Luke 1:28:

> "Hail, O favored one, the Lord is with you!"

This is the line that was rendered by Saint Jerome in the Vulgate:

> *"Ave, gratia plena, Dominus tecum"* — "Hail, full of grace, the Lord is with you."

Gabriel probably spoke to Mary in Aramaic, the spoken language of the Jews at that time. But Saint Luke records his words in Greek, and it's a bit difficult to render it smoothly in English. This is a woodenly literal translation:

> "Greetings, O-woman-who-has-been-graced, the Lord [be] with you!"

You will look in vain for an angelic greeting quite like this in the Bible. It is unusual for angels to praise those to whom they are sent. Usually, persons are called by their name or simply given a curt instruction. It does happen a couple times: the angel sent to Gideon calls him a "mighty warrior," but that might be angelic sarcasm, because Gideon is hiding in a wine press when he's discovered. Daniel (to whom Gabriel was also sent) is several times called "precious" or "valuable," using a Hebrew expression that is difficult to translate. But no angel calls a human being "graced" or "favored" prior to Mary.

In response to Mary's bewilderment at the greeting, Gabriel continues:

> "Do not be afraid Mary, for you have found favor [or grace] with God" (Luke 1:30).

Again, no angel ever declares anything approaching this to a human being in Scripture. The closest similar expressions are applied to Noah and Moses, both of whom are declared to have "found favor in the eyes of the Lord" (Gen 6:8; Exod 33:17). So, at the very least, Gabriel's greeting suggests Mary is on par with the savior of humanity (Noah) and the savior of Israel (Moses).

Then Gabriel goes on to declare Mary to be the future queen mother:

> "And behold, you will conceive in your womb and bear a son.... He will be great, and will be called the Son of the Most High; and the Lord God will give to him the throne of his father David, and he will reign over the house of Jacob for ever; and of his kingdom there will be no end." (Luke 1:31–33)[2]

The words of Gabriel are so familiar to us that we need to distance ourselves from them and hear them again as if for the first time. What would it mean for the status of this young girl from Nazareth that she is going to give birth to a son who is heir of the throne of David, an eternal reign over the kingdom of Israel (the "house of Jacob")? Especially when we recall that the Son of David was promised kingship not only over Israel but also over all the nations (Ps 2:8–12)? Gabriel is declaring to Mary that she is about to become the queen mother of the kingdom of Israel, and indeed, mother of the Emperor of the World!

We read the angelic message through the glasses of modern individualism, where family bonds are weak and poor. But in ancient times it was impossible for a woman to give birth to a son of such high status without her own status becoming exulted as well. Royal mothers and imperial mothers were women of great influence and respect. As we have seen, in the tradition of the Davidic monarchy, the mother of the king reigned as queen and served as intercessor for desperate suppliants.

So, is Gabriel showing honor or *venerating* Mary in this interaction? Indeed, he is! He addresses her in an unprecedented way:

---

2 The content of Gabriel's annunciation to Mary is a synopsis of the oracle that the prophet Nathan delivered to David in 2 Samuel 7 granting David a covenant with God forever. Jesus will be the fulfillment of the covenant promises to the House of David.

- As the first person declared "favored" or "graced" by an angel
- As the first *woman* in Scripture declared to be favored/graced by God
- As similar in some way to savior-figures like Noah and Moses

Then he goes on to declare her to be the future queen mother of Israel, whose son will be divine and royal, the international emperor from the line of David promised in Scripture. I would call that a pretty high honor.

Nor should we forget that he concludes by saying, "The Holy Spirit will come upon you, and the power of the Most High will overshadow you." The Holy Spirit only fell on prophets and other savior-figures in the Old Testament: in particular, David comes to mind. He received the Holy Spirit when anointed by Samuel (1 Sam 16). But "the power of the Most High will overshadow you" is completely unprecedented as a statement to any human being. The word used here is very rare;[3] it is used in Exodus 40:35 to describe the glory cloud of the divine presence overshadowing the Tabernacle. Gabriel is undeniably alluding to this event, comparing Mary to the Tabernacle of the Wilderness, the physical dwelling place of the divine presence!

Is Gabriel showing honor to Mary in saying this? Indeed, but we have moved far beyond those categories into the realm of mystery!

Summing Up the Bible and Mary

In summary, it was the Bible that helped me to "get" the doctrines about Mary.

Ironically, it was Revelation 12 and the vision of the mother of the Messiah as heavenly queen or even "queen of heaven" that first opened me up to the *possibility* that Scripture supported Catholic teachings.

---

3 The Greek verb *episkiazo*, "overshadow," occurs only four times in the Old Testament: Exod 40:35; Ps 90:4, 139:8; Prov 18:11.

The biblical doctrine of co-redemption, or the cooperation of the members of Christ with Christ's mission to redeem the world, enabled me to understand the idea of Mary as "Co-Redemptrix," especially in light of the biblical passages about her own "passion" (Luke 2:35; Rev 12:2).

Forced to lecture through the Bible, I "discovered" 1 Kings 2, the passage that most fully reveals the role of the queen mother in David's ancient kingdom. Having already realized that the Church was the transformed kingdom of David, Mary's role as venerated, enthroned intercessor in the heavenly court suddenly made sense.

Moving to the New Testament, I saw that key passages showed veneration of Mary already in Scripture, praising her absolutely unique role in salvation history in cooperation with her son.

The Bible praises Mary, the Church does, and so do I.

CHAPTER THREE

I Have a Confession to Make

The Sacrament of Reconciliation

It was probably the late summer of 1995, and I was driving past St. Alphonsus church near downtown when I had a sudden urge to pull into the parking lot and seek out a priest for confession.

That in itself may not strike you as hugely unusual. Surely it happens that people pass a church, are suddenly reminded of God, and also something on their conscience they would like to "unload." I'm sure I'm not the first person in history to have that experience.

What made it so unusual in my case was that, first of all, I wasn't Catholic. Second of all, I was the pastor of the little Protestant church about four blocks away.

So, why was a Protestant pastor wanting to confess his sins at a Catholic church, you might ask?

It started with a sermon series.

Protestant pastors usually do not have a lectionary to follow. Therefore, every Sunday one needs to choose the text (usually just one) to preach on. It can be daunting to pick a different random text each week, so like a lot of Protestant pastors, I simplified things by preaching through books of the Bible, at roughly the pace of half a chapter a week.

Anyway, I had preached through Philippians and Ephesians, and decided to tackle James, because James was very practical. Things went well through the first four chapters. But then I hit chapter 5 and this doozy of a passage:

> Is any one among you suffering? Let him pray. Is any cheerful? Let him sing praise. Is any among you sick? Let him call for the elders of the church, and let them pray over him, anointing him with oil in the name of the Lord;

and the prayer of faith will save the sick man, and the Lord will raise him up; and if he has committed sins, he will be forgiven. Therefore confess your sins to one another, and pray for one another, that you may be healed. The prayer of a righteous man has great power in its effects. (James 5:13–16)

The verse that really bothered me was verse 16: "Confess your sins to one another, and pray for one another, that you may be healed." It seemed very clear to me that James was connecting physical sickness with unconfessed sin; but it seemed narrow to limit the "healing" of which James speaks to only to the material realm. Wasn't it also spiritual healing that would result from confession and prayer?

This was what bothered me about the verse: *I had no real way to put it into practice in my congregation.* I prided myself in taking the Scriptures at face value and putting the literal meaning of God's word into practice. In the little downtown church that I pastored, I had very little oversight and a good deal of freedom to experiment with different forms of worship and church life. I really wanted to re-create, as much as possible, the "New Testament church" in my little neighborhood. According to James, the confession of sin was a hallmark of the "New Testament church." But we weren't doing it. So we weren't getting healed, either.

I looked out over my congregation and saw a lot of sickness, both physical and spiritual. There were spiritual ailments in my own life. In general, there seemed to be a lack of spiritual power among us, a kind of spiritual anemia. Was this because we didn't have the courage to put the words of Scripture into practice?

At the time, I could think of no workable way to implement the mutual confession of sin in my congregation. I pondered passing a mic around during our open "praise and prayer" times on Sunday morning, but the limitations of *that* were immediately obvious. Most people would not be comfortable baring their souls in front of the entire congregation. Furthermore, those who *were* comfortable doing so probably *shouldn't* because of all the scandalous information that would come out. In my few short years of ministry, there had already been some social disasters in which shocking or cringe-worthy things had come out during "praise and prayer" time. Sometimes this resulted in people leaving the church permanently.

Perhaps small groups? Maybe I could encourage the congregation to form groups of four or five who would gather in confidentiality to confess sin? This, too, would not work. There would still be the problem of discomfort and confidentiality. Things shared in small group would eventually get leaked and become known in the whole congregation. There was also the problem of bad counsel: perhaps some young Christian would share a sin on their conscience, and some older person in the group would misinform that it "wasn't really a sin" and "I do that all the time and it's okay."

Only in a group where there was a very high level of spiritual formation and maturity and a strong bond of confidentiality — like in a religious order — could mutual confession of sin really work. In the early churches to which Saint James wrote, there may have been this level of intensity, intimacy, and fervor. But that was not the case in my congregation or any congregation that I knew of.

That left me in a pickle because I had to preach on this text, and I didn't really know what to tell my congregation about it. I could hear my sermon now:

> "The Apostle James tells us to confess our sins to one another so that we can be healed, but we don't really have a way to do that, so I guess we'll all just have to stay sick."

That would be an inspiring message!

I had to figure out some way to preach on this text without actually encouraging the congregation to put it into practice; but I had to do so in such a way that it was not *obvious* that I was not encouraging them to practice it.

As all this was going through my head, my mind wandered to the practice of confession in the Catholic Church. I only knew a little about it, mostly from watching movies. I thought the introductory words were "Forgive me, Father, for I have sinned." Of course, I later found out it was "*Bless* me, Father, for I have sinned." Regardless, I began to ponder Catholic confession, and it occurred to me that the Catholics had figured out a way to put into practice what James was recommending in James 5:13–16, without the dangers posed by free-for-all public confession.

Interpreting Catholic practice through Protestant eyes, it seemed to me that Catholics had solved the problem by basically having everyone confess to their pastor in private. In a way, this was confession to the whole congregation, because the pastor was the spiritual head of the congregation. He represented the whole body. It was public in a way, because just by showing up for confession, people were visibly and publically admitting that they were sinners who needed to confess. But the content was kept private, to avoid all the damage that could be done to the penitent and others if certain things became public knowledge.

Furthermore, the pastor was supposed to be spiritually mature and well-trained in the Christian life. There wasn't much danger that he would misinform people about what was sinful and what wasn't. He was also in a position to give people advice about how to avoid sin in the future and live a more successful Christian life. Finally, the pastor was supposed to be a "righteous man" and an "elder" who could pray for his parishioners. James says right there in chapter 5 that the prayers of the "elders" and of "righteous men" are effective.

It bothered me that Catholics had a way to live out the literal meaning of God's word in James 5:13–16 but I, as a Protestant, didn't. I found that particularly ironic, because I prided myself in adherence to the "literal" meaning of Scripture and criticized the Catholic Church for avoiding it.

I have to explain, too, that the attitude I inherited from my parents about the Catholic Church had a kind of "split personality." On a theoretical level, we were intellectually committed to a radical rejection of Catholicism, to the point of regarding the Mass not only as bad Christian worship, but literally idolatrous. On the other hand, my father was a career naval chaplain and interacted on a daily basis with Catholic priest-chaplains, and as far as my memory serves, he had a high regard for most if not all of them. We even had priests over to our home for dinner periodically — friends of my father — and my mother had a high regard for many of them, too. One of my dad's closest professional friends was a priest named John O'Connor, who later was made a bishop, and eventually the Cardinal Archbishop of New York.

So, I grew up with this strange ambivalence about Catholicism. My father would mock the "bells and smells" and "superstition," but then remark about how only the Catholic chaplains had enough education to hold a decent theological conversation. My mother had a great admiration for Catholic moral theology, especially on life issues, because she had worked closely with the Bishop of Honolulu in the early days of the pro-life movement (we were stationed on Oahu when *Roe v. Wade* came out). She admired how much time the priests would spend in prayer (praying the liturgy of the hours) in contrast to Protestant chaplains, some of whom prayed very little. My mother also liked certain Catholic hymns and devotional practices, like midnight Mass on Christmas Eve, which she would occasionally attend. On certain issues, she would remark, "I think we threw the baby out with the bathwater at the Reformation."

That "split personality" was very present on that afternoon in 1995 as I passed by St. Alphonsus parish. How could a theoretically-very-anti-Catholic Protestant pastor have an urge to go confess to a Catholic priest? Simple: I wanted to live out James 5, and I knew Catholics had a way to do it. I was also, frankly, troubled by my own sins and my own inability to overcome patterns of sinfulness. I figured the reason I was mired in various bad habits was because I needed the "healing" that James said came from confession but I didn't have the courage to confess to anyone. In my defense, there was no good way to do so in my Protestant system. Furthermore, priests didn't scare me. I had known a lot of them as my dad's professional colleagues, and by and large I liked them. Like my parents, I had a high opinion of priests in person; just not on a theoretical level.

What happened? I lost my nerve. I knew the pastor of St. Alphonsus would probably talk to me even though I wasn't a Catholic, was unlikely to turn me away, and certainly would keep my confidence. Still, I was afraid one of my own congregation would see my car in the parking lot and get scandalized about what was going on. So, I never did pull into St. Alphonsus for confession. I figured out some way to subvert the force of James 5 in my sermon — I can't remember what I came up with — and I just moved on with my life, trying to put the awkward issue of confession behind me. But it came up again, later, in a different form.

One of the social challenges present in almost every urban community in America is rampant use of street drugs, and the neighborhood around my church was no different. Moreover, many spiritual writers have observed that there is a close connection between drug activity and spiritual warfare. One of the best-known Catholic writers on this subject, the late Father Gabrielle Amorth, one-time chief exorcist of Rome, wrote:

> Two evils are often tied to satanic rites: the legalization of abortion and the spread of illegal drugs.[1]

So it's not surprising that as I did pastoral care and evangelization in this neighborhood I ran into spiritual warfare issues. I encountered persons within my church and the broader community who had "problems" that were clearly beyond typical spiritual, psychological, or psychiatric categories. When I started running into this, I was out of my depth. The seminary I attended gave us little to no training in spiritual warfare or deliverance ministry. Some of the profs who had served as foreign missionaries had some experience of the occult on the mission field, but were not experts in the area. I needed help.

Thankfully, help came. Actually, one of my parishioners got frustrated with my ineffectiveness and started asking around among her Christian friends if there was anyone really good in deliverance ministry. She eventually happened upon Jim — not his real name — and in time she introduced Jim to me.

---

1   Gabrielle Amorth, *An Exorcist: More Stories* (Ignatius, 2002), 13.

Jim was a remarkable man, one of the most influential personalities in my life and spiritual development. He was a retired sales executive in his mid-seventies who looked and acted like someone in his early fifties. He had been involved in deliverance ministry ever since the charismatic revival that began in the 1970s, and over the years he had honed his approach. When we had gotten to know each other quite well, Jim shared with me that in the "early days," when he and his fellow deliverance ministers suspected the presence of evil spirits in a person's life, they would attempt a "power encounter." Similar to a formal exorcism in the Catholic tradition, they would call up the spirit(s) and attempt to drive him/them out by force in the name of Jesus.

Unfortunately, this method resulted in a lot of the supernatural phenomena that appear in your typical exorcism movie: superhuman strength, violence, cursing, and danger to everyone involved. So, Jim and his colleagues started searching for something better and safer. After thirty years, his methodology had become refined and looked very different.

I remember the first time I took an afflicted parishioner out to meet Jim. We drove to his house in the countryside, and Jim greeted us and welcomed us into his home. We made small talk while he prepared some soft drinks, and then we gathered around a table to "get down to business." Jim opened with a prayer, asking Jesus to bind any evil spirits that were present, so that they would keep silence and not interfere. Then, Jim brought out a large three-ring binder enclosing hundreds of pages of lists of sins, organized in seven different categories. Placing the binder open and in front of the afflicted person, Jim would begin working through the list. At each item, the question was the same: "Have you ever done this? If so, verbally confess and renounce before us as witnesses." The process took a long time — as much as two to three hours, occasionally taking breaks to get a drink or visit the restroom. When all the lists had been worked through, and the "deliveree" had confessed and renounced any sin or evil involvement that he or she could remember over the course of his/her lifetime, we prayed together again, and the process was over.

I found it to be very beneficial (I went through it myself as a trial) in my own spiritual life and saw good fruit from each of my parishioners who were willing to undergo the process. Jim explained that after years of trying different methods he found this process of thorough, audible confession in the presence of witnesses was the least traumatic for the person delivered, typically did not pose danger to others involved, and produced better and longer lasting freedom and peace — spiritual and psychological — than a "power encounter."

Well, what does that "process" sound like to you? Catholics reading this book may recognize it as, essentially, a non-sacramental general confession.[2] General confession is a lengthy confession involving a thorough review of one's life. Though uncommon in American Catholic circles in recent years, general confession has been warmly recommended as a periodic practice by several saints, most notably Francis de Sales and Ignatius of Loyola. Saint Ignatius recommended it on an annual basis as part of a retreat.

My friend Jim had found that such a thorough acknowledgment and renunciation of sin left evil spirits with essentially no handholds, no "grip" left on a person's soul. It seems to reduce the spirits to impotence, and they leave, either by force or voluntarily.

At the time I was working with Jim, Catholicism was not on my radar. The similarity of what we were doing and the sacrament of Reconciliation did not occur to me. Years later, though, after I had moved to Notre Dame and begun to consider more seriously the claims of the Catholic Church, the connection between sacramental confession and deliverance ministry flashed to mind very quickly. I perceived that confession was a form of pastoral care and deliverance, the "front lines" of the Church's

---

2   General confession is, of course, quite different from general absolution, with which it is sometimes confused. General absolution is a conditional grant of forgiveness of sins given by a priest to a group of Christians who are under some kind of duress that prevents the usual reception of the sacrament of Reconciliation (Confession). For example, a group of soldiers may be about to charge into battle where many are likely to lose their lives.

spiritual warfare. Confession had an exorcistic force. One should go into the confessional not to fulfill duty but to find freedom.

In later years, I have had the opportunity to discuss the relationship of confession to spiritual warfare with priest-exorcists, who have confirmed my perspective. For example, Father Amorth writes:

> In my experience, a good general confession — which I always recommend as a starting point — in conjunction with an intense life of prayer and grace, is sufficient to end the afflictions. Without prayer and grace, exorcisms are ineffective.[3]

Or again, answering a reader's question, he asserts:

> **Q.** My pastor claims the best exorcism is confession.
> **A.** He is right. It is the most direct means to fight Satan, because it is the sacrament that tears souls from the demon's grasp, strengthens against sin, unites us more closely to God, and helps conform our souls increasingly to the divine will. I advise frequent confession, possibly weekly, to all victims of evil activities."[4]

For myself, I do practice weekly confession, because as a teacher of Scripture and theology, I feel particularly vulnerable. I know that if I should fall into sin or under evil influence, I could do a lot of damage to many young people.

So, my sermon series on James lead to a long journey through the issue of confession that culminated with this sacrament being one of the biggest draws for me to enter the Catholic Church. One reason I became Catholic was to be able, on a regular basis, to live out the practice of "confessing your sins to one another" and receiving prayer and advice from a "righteous man" (James 5:16).

Of course, there were other passages of Scripture relevant to the sacrament of Reconciliation that I had overlooked, whose

---

3 Amorth, *Exorcist: More Stories*, 79.
4 Ibid., 195.

significance became apparent to me only much later, when I had the responsibility of teaching Scripture.

For example, in chapter one, on the papacy, we looked closely at Matthew 16:19 and the parallel in 18:18:

> "Whatever you bind on earth shall be bound in heaven, and whatever you loose on earth shall be loosed in heaven."

Earlier we said that the terms "bind" and "loose" had the sense in Jesus' day of making authoritative decisions about how to interpret divine law in daily living. That's true. But the terms also have a secondary sense of "forgive" ("loose") or "decline to forgive" ("bind"). Our Lord's words, which were spoken not to all disciples but to Peter and the apostles, invest the apostles with the authority to make decisions about the moral law, but also to forgive ("loose") those who violate that law. This is seen more clearly in a parallel passage from John 20:

> And when he had said this, he breathed on them, and said to them, "Receive the Holy Spirit. If you forgive the sins of any, they are forgiven; if you retain the sins of any, they are retained." (John 20:22–23)

John's phrase "If you forgive … if you retain," serves as an explanation for Matthew's "Whatever you bind … whatever you loose." In both instances, the apostles are granted the authority to forgive, or retain, sins.

I remember what I was taught in the Protestant seminary about John 20:23. The professor passed on John Calvin's interpretation. Calvin said this verse concerned preaching. It was through the preaching of the Gospel that the apostles would forgive and retain sin. The apostles would preach; those who received the message would be forgiven, and those who rejected it would not. Jesus meant nothing more than that.

I can agree that, in a secondary sense, there may be many ways that the apostles would mediate God's forgiveness of sin, and preaching the Gospel is certainly one of them. But one can clearly see that *preaching* cannot be the *primary* meaning of John 20:23, because there is nothing about preaching in the verse. Any ideas of preaching have to be *imported* into the text; they do not arise out of it. As always, the best form of biblical interpretation is to allow the meaning to come out of the text (*exegesis*), not push the meaning into the text (*eisegesis*).

Jesus says, "Whose sins you forgive … whose sins you retain." This implies the apostles will make an intentional decision whether to forgive or retain the sins of others. That's the plain sense of the text. To reduce it merely to preaching removes the action of forgiving and retaining. In such a scenario, the apostles never make a conscious decision to forgive or retain, but merely a decision to preach. Surely, if that is what Jesus meant, he could have said, "Receive the Holy Spirit. You will preach, and others will be forgiven or not, as they receive or resist your message."

But Jesus' actual words clearly indicate that he is investing the apostles to make decisions about forgiving or retaining the sins of others. How will they find out about other's sins in order to make a decision? Presumably, others will tell them of their sins, and they will make a decision to forgive or retain. That is the basic form of the sacrament of Confession to this day. A believer goes to a successor of the apostles — or someone authorized by him — recounts his or her sins, and receives a judgment (almost always favorable) about whether they are forgiven or retained.

In doing so, the apostles and their successors are actually fulfilling the role of the priesthood of the Old Testament. It is a little-noticed fact that the Old Testament *also* had a form of the sacrament of Confession, and the priests administered it. After giving a lengthy list of possible sins, the book of Leviticus says:

> When a man is guilty in any of these, he shall *confess* the sin he has committed, and he shall bring his guilt offering to the LORD for the sin which he has committed, a female from the flock, a lamb or a goat, for a sin offering; and the *priest* shall make atonement for him for his sin. (Lev 5:5–6, emphasis added)

"He shall confess the sin he has committed," the Bible says. To whom? The text doesn't say explicitly, but upon reflection it becomes obvious to whom: to the priest, because the priest needs to ensure that the sacrificial animal he brings to the sanctuary fits the sin he committed. The required sacrifice varied considerably depending on the kind of offense and the wealth of the worshiper. It was the priest's responsibility to make sure all complied with God's law. Thus, he had to know what the sin was.

It was the priest who mediated forgiveness to the worshiper. A frequent refrain in Leviticus is the following line:

> "The priest shall make atonement for him for the sin which he has committed, and he shall be forgiven." (Lev 5:10, cf. 4:20, 26, 31, 35, 5:13, 16, 18, 6:7, 19:22; Num 15:25, 28)

Forgiveness of sins was duty of the priest — not the prophet, the sage, the king, the judge, or any other office in ancient Israel.

There is a theme in the New Testament of the apostles taking over for the Old Testament priesthood — indeed, the apostles becoming "New Covenant priests." In chapter five, we will examine this theme in greater detail. For now, it's enough to observe that Jesus' gift of the Holy Spirit to the apostles together with the command, "Whose sins you forgive are forgiven them; whose sins you retain are retained," is a conferral upon them of *priestly* responsibility.

Now, some of my readers may be willing to agree that Jesus gave the apostles the authority to do something like confession. Nonetheless, they will object to the idea that this authority was passed on to the successors of the apostles, those who took over their roles of leadership when they died.

I have three responses to that objection: one from logic, one from history, and one from Scripture.

First, from logic. If Jesus was establishing his church to last for many generations, why would he give the power to forgive or retain sin only to the first generation of leaders? Would this great gift to the Church suddenly become unnecessary after thirty years? It doesn't make sense. Building on this point, let's keep in mind that the Gospel of John, by anyone's best estimate, was written late in John's life, when he was the last apostle still alive, and his own death seemed imminent, probably around A.D. 95.

Why would John record Jesus commissioning the apostles to forgive or retain sin (John 20:23) if it had no relevance to his readers?

Think about it: by the time his Gospel was published, all the apostles invested with this power were dead or soon would be. Was John's only point in John 20:23 that the apostles once had an awesome power that was completely gone now? I highly doubt it. I believe John 20:23 was meant to be relevant for all time. I believe John records the commissioning to forgive and retain sin (20:23) to inform the current and future generations of Christians about the origin of the power of absolution that was given to the leadership of the Church: the apostles and those who succeeded them.

Second, from history. What did the early Christians think? Did they believe the authority of the apostles died with them or that it passed to their successors? I think the testimony is clear: the early Christians understood that the authority to lead the Church of Christ was passed from the apostles to the bishops and presbyters they appointed, and so on down to the present age. Clement, the bishop of Rome, who was himself ordained by Peter, wrote the following around A.D. 80 (probably before the Gospel of John was even published!):

> Through countryside and city [the apostles] preached, and they appointed their earliest converts, testing them by the Spirit, to be the bishops and deacons of future believers.... Our apostles knew through our Lord Jesus Christ that there would be strife for the office of bishop. For this reason, therefore, having received perfect fore-knowledge, they appointed those who have already been mentioned and afterwards added the further provision that, if they should die, other approved men should succeed to their ministry.[5]

Likewise, another early Father, Irenaeus, writing about a hundred years later, writes to defend the legitimacy of the Church:

---

5 *Letter to the Corinthians* 42:4–5, 44:1–3 [A.D. 80].

We are in a position to enumerate those who were instituted bishops by the apostles and their successors down to our own times.[6]

Saint Gregory the Great, bishop of Rome, comments the following on John 20:23 in the A.D. 500s:

[The apostles] are admitted to the powers of the supreme Judgment-seat; so that, in the place of God, they retain some men's sins, and remit others. Their place in the church, the bishops now hold; who receive the authority to bind [cf. Matt 18:18], when they are admitted to the rank of government.[7]

(Anyone who wants to read more about the idea of succession and the authority of the apostles passing to their successors, please see chapter five, on the priesthood.)

Third, from Scripture. All the biblical models and background for the role of the apostles suggests that they held an office whose authority would be passed on to others after their death.

The ministry of the forgiveness of sins in the Old Testament was entrusted to the priests, who held an office that passed to others after their death or retirement. Furthermore, the power of "binding" and "loosing" that Jesus entrusts to the apostles (Matt 18:18) had previously been exercised by the scribes and Pharisees (Matt 23:4) who "sat in Moses' seat" (Matt 23:2–3), that is, were successors of Moses and heirs to his authority. In Judaism, the rabbis of each generation had the authority to "bind and loose" for that generation of Jews.[8] But Jesus replaces the "seat of Moses" (Matt 23:2) with "thrones" for the apostles (Matt 19:28), drawing on the principle of the "thrones of the House of David" (Ps 122:5).

---

6   *Against Heresies* 3:3:1 [A.D. 189].

7   Excerpt of Saint Gregory the Great, Homily XXVI, from Thomas Aquinas, J. H. Newman (ed.), *Catena Aurea: Commentary on the Four Gospels, Collected out of the Works of the Fathers, Volume 4: St. John* (Oxford: John Henry Parker, 1845), 608; commenting on John 20:23.

8   See Kaufmann Kohler, "Binding and Loosing," *The Jewish Encyclopedia* (New York: Ktav, 1906), http://www.jewishencyclopedia.com/articles/3307-binding-and-loosing.

When Jesus speaks of the apostles occupying "thrones" (Matt 19:28; Luke 22:30), it implies an enduring position to be filled by another upon death, just as the throne of a prince or king is filled by his heir after his death. This is clearest with respect to Peter: Jesus entrusts to him the office of royal steward (Matt 16:18–19), which was a continuing office with successors in the Old Testament (Isa 22:19-21).

When Judas died, Peter spoke of the need for another to fill his "office" and "station" (Acts 1:20). Even within the New Testament itself, we observe the apostles appointing others to exercise their authority on their behalf in their absence. Thus, Paul writes to Titus: "This is why I left you in Crete, that you might amend what was defective, and *appoint elders in every town* as I directed you" (Titus 1:5). Consequently, Titus acts on Paul's behalf when Paul can't be there in person. The appointing of elders was originally the prerogative of the apostles themselves (Acts 14:23), but now Paul has delegated it to Titus. Thus, we see the apostles transmitting their authority to others even within the pages of Scripture. This is why Saint Gregory can so confidently assert about the apostles, "Their place in the Church is now held by the bishops, who receive the authority to 'bind,' when they are admitted to the rank of government." [9]

We'll leave off the discussion of apostolic succession at this point, because we will be treating it more in chapter five on the priesthood.

Let's just sum up what we have covered concerning confession.

The Bible recommends the confession of sin to another believer(s) and seeking prayers for healing from "elders" (*presbuteroi*) and righteous men (James 5:14–16). Even if it were nothing else, the sacrament of Reconciliation is a practical, workable way of living out James' exhortation.

Confession of sin also has exorcistic power, and can be viewed primarily as a very effective form of deliverance ministry.

---

9 Saint Gregory the Great, Homily XXVI, from Aquinas, Newman (ed.), *Catena Aurea*, 608; commenting on John 20:23.

Jesus established the essential principle of the sacrament of Reconciliation when he conferred on the apostles the power to "bind and loose" (Matt 16:18–19, 18:18) and to "forgive and retain" sins (John 20:23). Scholars recognize these two commissions are interrelated. [10] The natural sense of the text is that the apostles were authorized to hear the sins of others and to make a judgment about whether or not to absolve them. Biblical principles from the Old Testament, as well as key texts from the New Testament, indicate the authority of the apostles was *intended* to be passed on, and was *in fact* passed on. The early Fathers confirm this.

---

10   See Kaufmann Kohler, "Binding and Loosing," *The Jewish Encyclopedia* (New York: Ktav, 1906), http://www.jewishencyclopedia.com/articles/3307-binding-and-loosing.

CHAPTER FOUR

"Mass" Conversion

The Eucharist, the Bible, and Me

Even with two master's degrees from one of the most rigorous Protestant seminaries in America, I did not fully understand what the word "Eucharist" meant. We didn't use the word in my branch of Protestantism. Instead, we talked about "the Lord's Supper" and "Communion."

When I first began working as an urban pastor, I was pretty casual about scheduling the "Lord's Supper" for my congregation. Our religious tradition, in practice, did not put much emphasis on "sacraments." Preaching and doctrine were much more important.

Interestingly, however, as the years passed in urban ministry, and my co-pastor and I looked at the biblical texts concerning the Lord's Supper more closely, we began to treat it with much greater seriousness. We scheduled one celebration a month, and tried to observe it with as much dignity as our humble inner-city congregation could muster.

Still, we didn't have much of a theology of the Lord's Supper. If you had asked me what was going on, I would have talked about symbolism, remembrance, and a certain "special presence" of Jesus during the communion service. We knew it was important because Jesus said to do it (Lk 22:19) and Paul said you could die for doing it wrong (1 Cor 11:30). But beyond that, it was pretty vague.

When I first started having serious conversations with theologically literate Catholics at Notre Dame, they would bring up the topic of the Eucharist, but I wasn't interested in discussing it. I wanted to debate about *sola fide* or *sola scriptura*. After a while, it began to dawn on me that Protestants don't just differ with the Catholic Church about various particular doctrines, they don't even agree about *which doctrines are central and which are peripheral!*

I had not been exposed to the doctrine of the Real Presence growing up. It wasn't really on my "radar screen" as an important Catholic-Protestant issue of division. More pressing to me were questions regarding the role of faith and works in the doctrine of justification. To me and to many Protestants, the sacraments were peripheral, but doctrines like predestination were central. How completely upside down from a Catholic perspective! I came to realize that, for most Christians throughout history, *sacraments* were always central, and the doctrine of predestination was so peripheral the Church has never found it necessary to clearly define just one understanding of it.

In Catholicism, the Eucharist is the "source and summit of the Christian life" (CCC 1324), and the early Christian slogan, "The Eucharist makes the Christian and the Christian makes the Eucharist" is often quoted.[1] To me and to other Protestants, this made no sense at all. How could a little ceremony we observed as infrequently as three times a year possibly be central to the Christian life? To us, it was the Bible that was the "source and summit" of Christian life, and Catholics had usurped the role of God's Word with their "sacramentalism."

My Catholic friends tried to share with me scriptural testimony about the Eucharist, but none of it got through to me. Michael pointed me to portions of John 6, such as "unless you eat the flesh of the Son of Man and drink his blood, you have no life in you," but I was unimpressed. "All symbolic," was my response. When I read over John 6 carefully, everything seemed to be metaphorical to me. "'Eating his flesh and drinking his

---

1 This is from the record of the martyrdom of the forty-nine Christians of Abitene who were executed by Emperor Diocletian for holding to the Christian faith. The author of the account of the martyrdom digresses at one point to comment: "Don't you know, Satan, that it is the Sunday Eucharist which makes the Christian and the Christian that makes the Sunday Eucharist, so that one cannot subsist without the other, and vice versa?" Quoted by Pope Benedict XVI, Homily, May 29, 2005, http://www.vatican.va/holy_father/benedict_xvi/homilies/2005/documents/hf_ben-xvi_hom_20050529_bari_en.html.

blood' is just metaphor for receiving him as Lord and Savior," I thought. For me, it was the same for all the other blunt statements in John 6.

My Catholic friends would point out: "But when the crowd understands him literally, Jesus does not correct them and say, 'It was just a metaphor.'" "No," I would respond, "because he wanted to get rid of that crowd. He was trying to gross them out so that they would leave and let him get on with his retreat with the twelve disciples."

I was impervious to the witness of John 6. It was the same for all the other biblical testimonies the Eucharist: the Institution narratives (Matt 26:26–28; Mark 14:22–24; Luke 22:19–20; 1 Cor 10–11). "All metaphors," I would think, "Jesus calls himself a Rock, Jesus calls himself the Gate of the Sheep (Jn 10:7), and none of those are literal. Neither does he mean that bread is actually his body or wine is actually his blood."

My outlook was like a seamless suit of body armor that no scriptural text could penetrate. Someone had to give me a body blow that would crack my metaphorical armor and let some Eucharistic reality seep in. That someone turned out to be a Church Father.

As I recounted in the story of my own personal conversion journey, there did come a point in my theological conversations with Michael when we could not resolve our remaining disagreements by Scripture alone. The Eucharist was one of them. We both looked at the same texts. Michael insisted, "The plain meaning of the text is that the Eucharist simply *is* his body"; and I kept insisting, "You are overreading a figure of speech."

At this point, Michael suggested we start delving into the Church Fathers, to see how they interpreted Scripture. Surely the Fathers, being closer in time to Jesus and the apostles, and living in an age of purer faith, would have a better idea of what the Scriptures really meant. Whoever could show that his views were consistent with the Church Fathers was more likely to be correct. We agreed on this. That sounded fine to me, because I was convinced the Church Fathers were really Calvinists. Mike, however, knew what the Church Fathers were actually like, and I did not (I had never read any of them extensively except Augustine).

Believing they would confirm my interpretations of Scripture, I purchased a copy of the earliest writings of the Fathers (the "Apostolic Fathers"[2]), and jumped in with gusto, only to be surprised by what I found (and didn't find)!

I read *1 Clement* first, the letter from Clement, bishop of Rome, to the Church in Corinth, from around A.D. 80, while Saint John the Apostle was probably still alive. Clement's letter illustrated my earlier point about Protestants and Catholics *not even agreeing on what was important.* I was sure that Clement would use this early letter to the Corinthian Christians to reaffirm the core Christian doctrines: the Bible alone; faith alone; predestination. Instead, it was all about "peripheral" matters: visible unity of the Church; moral living; faithfulness and obedience to the visible office-bearers of the Church. He even had a strong endorsement of the principle of apostolic succession!

Clement shook me up, but it was really Ignatius of Antioch that broke me. When I started reading his seven letters to the seven churches of Asia Minor, I grew increasingly nervous. His stress on the authority of the local bishop, the importance of the roles of priests (*presbuteroi*) and deacons (*diakonoi*), and the visible unity of the Church all struck me as very "Catholic." In fact, he used the term "Catholic Church," which I had thought was a medieval innovation![3]

But it was his testimony in his *Letter to the Smyrneans,* chapters 6–7, that busted through my "body armor" and opened me up to see what the Scriptures were really saying about the Eucharist:

> Now note well those who hold heretical opinions about the grace of Jesus Christ which came to us; note how contrary they are to the mind of God. They have no concern for love, none for the widow, none for the orphan,

---

2 The Apostolic Fathers were the first generation of Church Fathers, so called because they were in living contact with the Apostles, and thus "Apostolic."

3 "Wherever the bishop appears, there let the congregation be; just as wherever Jesus Christ is, there is the catholic church" (Ignatius of Antioch, A.D. 106, *Letter to the Smyrneans* 8:2).

none for the oppressed, none for the prisoner or the one released, none for the hungry or thirsty. They abstain from the Eucharist and prayer, because they refuse to acknowledge that the Eucharist is the flesh of our Savior Jesus Christ, which suffered for our sins and which the Father by his goodness raised up. Therefore, those who deny the good gift of God perish in their contentiousness. It would be more to their advantage to love, in order that they might also rise up. It is proper, therefore, to avoid such people and not speak about them either privately or publicly.[4]

Reading this was a bit of a shock for me. I read and re-read the passage several times and finally said to myself, "There's no way to get a symbolic interpretation out of this passage." Ignatius was pastor of all the Christians in the city of Antioch. He was arrested and sent to Rome for execution around A.D. 106. He died being fed to lions in the Coliseum. He knew he was headed to his death when he wrote these letters, so he had no ulterior motives and nothing to gain for himself in this life.

Ignatius's testimony about the Eucharist was striking and frightening. The heretics, Ignatius says, "refuse to acknowledge that the Eucharist is the *flesh* of our savior Jesus Christ, which suffered for our sins and which the Father by his goodness raised up." Note that Ignatius does not say, "They deny that the Eucharist is our savior Jesus Christ, *who* suffered for our sins, and *whom* the Father raised up." He is much more graphic and physical. The Eucharist is "the flesh ... *which* suffered ... and the Father raised up." It's not "who" but "which." It's not just Jesus, but Jesus' body. In other words, it's not that the heretics deny that there is some mystical identity between the Eucharist and Jesus, it's that they will not go all the way and recognize it as Jesus' material *flesh*.

Ignatius's statement *will not* permit some kind of symbolic or metaphorical interpretation. He is, in fact, expressly rejecting a metaphorical or symbolic understanding of the Eucharist as a heresy. No, the Eucharist *is* Jesus' material body, the same Body that suffered and was resurrected. This is the faith of the Christian Church, as witnessed by one of the earliest postapostolic pastors, one who sealed his faith with martyrdom.

I'll explain the logic by which this passage broke me open to read the New Testament with new eyes:

1. Ignatius knew the Apostle John.
2. John probably died in A.D. 96 or so, about ten years before Ignatius wrote these words about the Eucharist.
3. Ignatius *must* have received instruction about the Eucharist from John himself, possibly from other apostles as well, since he lived in the same region of Asia Minor.
4. Ten years is too short a time for him to have gotten confused about the doctrine.
5. His willing acceptance of martyrdom pretty much rules out the possibility that he was trying to deceive the Christians of Smyrna and elsewhere about Eucharistic doctrine.
6. Therefore: If he wasn't confused and he wasn't lying, his simple identification of the Eucharist as the flesh of Jesus must be the teaching of the original apostles themselves!

(Now, I've had non-Catholic friends look at this passage and just tell me, "Well, Ignatius is wrong." My internal response has always been, "Okay, and who are you, two thousand years later and not facing martyrdom, to declare that one of the first pastors of the Church, who was instructed by the apostles themselves, is *wrong* about a central teaching of Christianity? Why should I believe *you* rather than Ignatius?")

After reading this passage of Ignatius of Antioch, I went *back* to the New Testament passages on the Eucharist, and it dawned on me meaningfully for the first time that the plain sense of all the Eucharistic passages was a simple *identity* between the Eucharistic bread and the Body of Jesus.

What does Jesus say at the Last Supper?

According to Matthew: "Take, eat, this is my body.... This is my blood of the covenant" (Matt 26:26, 28).

According to Mark: "Take; this is my body.... This is my blood of the covenant" (Mark 14:22, 24).

According to Luke: "This is my body which is given for you.... This cup ... is the new covenant in my blood" (Lk 22:19–20).

Are we going to respond to all this scriptural testimony by saying as Bill Clinton famously did, "What do you mean by 'is'?"

How about Saint Paul's testimony? Does he explain that Jesus meant this all as a metaphor? Far from it!

> For I received from the Lord what I also delivered to you, that the Lord Jesus on the night when he was betrayed took bread ... and said, "This *is* my body which is for you." ... In the same way also the chalice ... saying, "This chalice *is* the new covenant in my blood." (1 Cor 11:23, emphasis added)

Saint Paul follows up with two statements that confirm the "Real Presence" or true identity of the Eucharist with Christ's material body and blood.

First, he says:

> Whoever, therefore, eats the bread or drinks the cup of the Lord in an unworthy manner will be guilty of the body and blood of the Lord. (1 Cor 11:27)

Saint Paul uses a very strong phrase, "*guilty* of the body and blood of the Lord." The term "guilty" (Greek *enochos*) was consistently used in the Greek translation of the Old Testament (the Septuagint) to translate the Hebrew idiom, "His blood shall be upon him" (cf. Lev 20:9), meaning, "he is guilty of a crime so grave that the person who kills him will not be guilty of his death," or simply, "guilty of a capital crime."

If the Eucharistic bread and wine were mere symbols, unworthy use of them would be bad, to be sure — but it is hard to see that it would be *a capital crime*. That would seem to require some *direct* profanation of the Body and Blood of Christ himself.

Next, Saint Paul says:

> Let a man examine himself, and so eat of the bread and drink of the cup. For anyone who eats and drinks with-

out recognizing [Greek *diakrino*] the body eats and drinks judgment upon himself. (1 Cor 11:28–29)

I remember struggling with this passage in New Testament exegesis class. Our seminary professor admitted uncertainty about what the phrase "recognizing [Greek *diakrino*] the body" meant. He suggested it expressed a failure to recognize that the Christian congregation was the mystical Body of Christ. This interpretation seemed like a stretch then, and I still feel it is a stretch: it doesn't fit the context, which is concerning the reality of Christ's presence *in the bread and wine.*

But of course, in that seminary classroom, we *could not* come up with the correct understanding of this passage because we were doctrinally committed to *denying* what Saint Paul says here. Because what he means is, "Anyone who eats and drinks without recognizing [that it is] the body [of Christ] eats and drinks judgment upon himself." In other words, those who receive communion casually, in a state of sin, just don't realize that they are actually taking the Body and Blood of Christ into themselves. They probably think they are just participating in some *symbolic act* in which it doesn't matter what their actual *spiritual condition* is when they partake.

Paul follows up with this frightening statement:

That is why many of you are weak and ill, and some have died. (1 Cor 11:30)

Saint Paul asserts that unworthy reception of the Eucharist can be fatal. This makes perfect sense based on his use of the word *enochos*, "guilty of capital offense," when describing unworthy reception as "guilty of the body and blood of the Lord." In the Old Testament, the *enochos* person had to be executed. Saint Paul is asserting that the Holy Spirit is executing judgment on the *enochos* persons in the Corinthian congregation who are partaking unworthily.

Throughout history, the Church has periodically *excommunicated* public sinners from Eucharistic participation *for their own safety*, because the Church does not want these sinners to die by divine judgment. (In recent decades, excommunication has become very uncommon, apparently because the authorities of the Church wish to leave judgment on public, blatant sinners directly in the hands of God.)

Finally, let's look at the classic Eucharistic text of John 6:

> After this Jesus went to the other side of the Sea of Galilee.… And a multitude followed him.… Jesus went up on the mountain, and there sat down with his disciples. Now the Passover, the feast of the Jews, was at hand.… One of his disciples, Andrew, Simon Peter's brother, said to him, "There is a lad here who has five barley loaves and two fish; but what are they among so many?" Jesus said, "Make the people lie down [Greek *anapipto*]." Now there was much grass in the place; so the men reclined [*anapipto*], in number about five thousand. Jesus then took [*lambano*] the loaves [*arton*], and when he had given thanks [*eucharistein*], he distributed [*didomi*] them to those who were reclined [*anakeimenos*]; so also the fish, as much as they wanted. And when they had eaten their fill, he told his disciples, "Gather up the left over fragments [*klasmata*, "breakings"], that nothing may be lost." So they gathered them up and filled twelve baskets with fragments from the five barley loaves, left by those who had eaten. (John 6:1–13)

Like most Protestants, I used to deny that this passage had any connection with the Eucharist. However, I had never studied the passage in depth, either. Once one does that, it's impossible to deny that John makes a Eucharistic connection here, because he purposely uses terms that call to mind the Eucharistic Institution narratives of the other Gospels in addition to his own account of the Last Supper.

First of all, notice that John records Jesus performing this miracle on the Passover (Jn 6:4), the feast on which the Last Supper would later take place (Mt 26:17). Secondly, note that the occasion for the miracle is Jesus sitting down on a mountain with his disciples (6:3), just as later, he will sit down with his disciples on Mt. Zion to celebrate the Last Supper (cf. Lk 22:30). Thirdly, note that Jesus commands the people to "lie down" (Greek *anapipto*). The only other times this verb occurs in the Gospel of John are in reference to Jesus (13:12) and the apostle John (13:25, 21:20) reclining at the Last Supper. Fourthly, note that at the heart of the miracle account (v. 11), John describes Jesus multiplying the loaves by using five words that occur in the Last Supper/Institution narratives of the other Gospels: take (*lambano*), loaf/bread (*arton*), give thanks (*eucharisteo*), give/distribute (*didomi*), and recline (*anakeimenos*). Then, he describes the bread that remains after everyone has eaten using the rare word *klasmata*, literally "breakings," which echoes the Last Supper accounts that speak of Jesus "breaking" the bread.

Common Words in John 6 and the Institution Narratives				
John 6:11–12	*Matthew 26*	*Mark 14*	*Luke 22*	*Paul (1 Cor 11)*
Take/*lambano*	v. 26	v. 22	v. 19	v. 23
Bread/*arton*	v. 26	v. 22	v. 19	v. 23
Give thanks/ *Eucharistein*	v. 27	v. 23	v. 19	v. 24
Give/*didomi*	vv. 26, 27	vv. 22, 23	v. 19	--
Recline/ *anakeimenos*	v. 20	v. 18	v. 27	--
Break/breakings *klao/klasmata*	v. 26	v. 22	v. 19	v. 24

In the discourse that follows (John 6:16–71), more themes from the Last Supper/ Institution of the Eucharist crop up. Jesus discusses the idea of *eating his flesh* and *drinking his blood*, and the only other places in the New Testament where eating Jesus' body and blood are mentioned are in the Last Supper accounts of Matthew, Mark, Luke, and Paul. In particular, nothing in John 6 prepares the reader for the introduction of the idea of "drinking blood" in verse 53, and it adds nothing to the discourse *except* to reinforce the Eucharistic interpretation of his words. Jesus also discusses his desertion by his own disciples (vv. 60–66) and predicts the betrayal by Judas (vv. 70–71), both of which are major themes in the Gospel accounts of the Last Supper.

Common Themes in John 6 and the Institution Narratives				
John 6	*Matthew 26*	*Mark 14*	*Luke 22*	*Paul (1 Cor 11)*
Eating Jesus' flesh (Greek *phago sarx*) (vv. 51–53, 56)	v. 26	v. 22	v. 19	v. 24
Drinking Jesus' blood (Greek *pino haima*) (vv. 53–54, 56)	vv. 27–28	v. 23–24	v. 20	v. 25
Desertion of the Disciples (vv. 60–66)	vv. 31–35	vv. 26–31	vv. 31–34	cf. vv. 17–22
Betrayal by Judas (v. 70–71)	vv. 21–25	vv. 18–21	vv. 21–23	cf. vv. 27–32!

One can't reasonably argue that all the connections between John 6 and the accounts of the Last Supper and the Institution of the Eucharist are merely coincidental. Any trained Bible scholar will concede that, by the standards of modern biblical exegesis, one must acknowledge a connection. The connection is not subtle. The first Christian readers and hearers of John's Gospel would have had to be *tone deaf* not to recognize the common language and themes between John 6 and the Institution narratives! After all, the Institution narrative, in one of its variations, was recited every week at the primitive Eucharistic celebrations of the early Church!

Justin Martyr gives us one of our earliest descriptions of Christian worship in A.D. 150:

> And on the day called Sunday, all who live in cities or in the country gather together to one place, and *the memoirs of the apostles* [i.e., the Gospels] or *the writings of the prophets* [i.e., the Old Testament] are read, as long as time

permits; then, when the reader has ceased, the president verbally instructs, and exhorts to the imitation of these good things. Then we all rise together and pray, and, as we before said, when our prayer is ended, bread and wine and water are brought, and the president in like manner offers prayers and thanksgivings, according to his ability, and the people assent, saying "Amen"; and there is a distribution to each, and a partaking of the *eucharisted* things, and to those who are absent a portion is sent by the deacons.[5]

So, we know from the earliest times it was the custom to read the Gospels ("the memoirs of the apostles") at the Eucharistic celebration (now called Mass). Observe what Justin further says about the Eucharist and the Gospels:

And this food is called among us *eucharistia*, of which no one is allowed to partake but the man who believes that the things that we teach are true.… For not as common bread and common drink do we receive these; but … we have been taught that the food which is blessed by the prayer of His word, and from which our blood and flesh by transmutation are nourished, *is the flesh* [Greek *sarx*] *and blood* [Greek *haima*] *of that Jesus* who was made flesh.[6] For the apostles, in the memoirs composed by them, *which are called Gospels*, have thus delivered unto us what was enjoined upon them; that Jesus took bread, and

---

5   Justin Martyr, "The First Apology of Justin," A. Roberts, J. Donaldson, and A. C. Coxe (Eds.), *The Ante-Nicene Fathers: The Apostolic Fathers with Justin Martyr and Irenaeus, Vol. 1* (Buffalo, NY: Christian Literature Company, 1885), 186. Emphasis mine.

6   Justin alludes to the Gospel of John here. "That Jesus who was made flesh" is an allusion to John 1:14: "The Word was made flesh and dwelt among us." The phrase "flesh and blood of Jesus" is an allusion to various passages of John 6 (e.g., v. 53, "Unless you eat my flesh and drink my blood you have not life in you"), because John *alone* of the Gospel writers uses the combination "flesh and blood" (Greek *sarx kai haima*) whereas the other Gospels use the pair "body and blood" (Greek *soma kai haima*).

when He had given thanks, said, "This do in remembrance of Me, this is My body"; and that, after the same manner, having taken the cup and given thanks, He said, "This is My blood"; and gave it to them alone.

Now, I ask every contemporary Christian to ponder the following scenario: When the early Christians gathered on the first day of the week for the Eucharistic celebration as Justin Martyr describes, and they read "the memoir of the Apostle John," or the Gospel of John, and came to the following passage —

> So Jesus said to them, "Truly, truly, I say to you, unless you eat the flesh of the Son of man and drink his blood, you have no life in you; he who eats my flesh and drinks my blood has eternal life, and I will raise him up at the last day." (John 6:53–54)

— is it plausible that they would *not* see the obvious line of connection to the Eucharist they were about to consume? I don't think so.

I submit to you that there is *no way* the early Christians *did not* read John 6 in a Eucharistic sense, since they habitually read the Gospel *at the Eucharistic celebration!*[7] Moreover, I submit to you there is *no way* the author of the Gospel *did* NOT *realize* how his words would be understood by early Christians. In other words, John had to have known the early Christian community would understand John 6 to be stressing the necessity of Eucharistic communion, and therefore *must have intended* the text to communicate that point. Both as a scholar and a believer, I find this argument — the argument from the early Christian community's understanding of John 6 — to be the most compelling reason for accepting the Bread of Life discourse in John 6 as, ultimately, a statement concerning the Eucharist.

---

7   One needs to remember that the early Christians were largely poor persons, and the vast majority did not have the money to afford to buy books, even if they could read. Christians did not own their own Bibles — they were dependent on the public reading of Scripture at the gathering of the Christian community, which took place on a weekly basis when everyone gathered for the Eucharistic celebration.

I know about attempts to argue that "eating [Jesus'] flesh and blood" are just metaphors for believing in Jesus. But the concept of eating flesh and blood is universally negative in the Old Testament. Take the time to look up the passages where "eating flesh and blood" are described. You will find it's either forbidden (Gen 9:4; Deut 12:16, 23) or being used as an idiom for the repulsive violence of warfare and judgment (Deut 32:43; Isa 49:26; Jer 46:10; Ezek 39:17). It's highly unlikely that Jesus would pick such a negative concept to be used as a metaphor for something like "trust" or "faith" when speaking to the Jews who knew the Scriptures.

Moreover, the direction of Jesus' argument in John 6 does not move toward metaphor, but rather toward physicality. Jesus becomes more concrete, not less so, in the course of the chapter. For example, as the Bread of Life discourse moves to its conclusion, Jesus stops using the general Greek word "to eat" (*esthio* or *phago*, depending on tense) and adopts the Greek word for "munch, chew, gnaw," which is *trogo*. Here is the climactic passage of the Bread of Life discourse translated to bring out the force of the Greek verb:

> So Jesus said to them, "Truly, truly, I say to you, unless you *chew* [Greek *trogo*] the flesh of the Son of man and drink his blood, you have no life in you; he who *chews* my flesh and drinks my blood has eternal life, and I will raise him up at the last day. For my flesh is food indeed, and my blood is drink indeed. He who *chews* my flesh and drinks my blood abides in me, and I in him. As the living Father sent me, and I live because of the Father, so he who *chews* me will live because of me. This is the bread which came down from heaven, not such as the fathers ate and died; he who *chews* this bread will live forever." (John 6:53–58)

Note how emphatic Jesus is. *Four times* (vv. 53, 54, 57, and 58) he repeats essentially the same point: "You need to chew my flesh to live forever." A purely symbolic sense seems excluded by verse 55: "For my flesh is true food, and my blood is true drink."

The crowds in John 6 understand Jesus in a literal sense (John 6:60, 66), and Jesus does not bother to correct them. Yet elsewhere in the Gospels, when Jesus is misunderstood, he either expresses frustration at the misunderstanding (John 3:10), or redirects the conversation (John 4:15–16), or clarifies his metaphor (Matt 16:11–12). Jesus gives no indication that the crowds are misunderstanding him; only that they are not believing his message (John 6:61–65).

Many attempt to take Jesus' statement in John 6:65 — "It is the Spirit that gives life, the flesh is of no avail" — as undercutting any physical, material, or sacramental understanding of Jesus' words. The fundamental point such persons fail to realize is that Jesus says "*the* flesh is of no avail," not "*my* flesh is of no avail"; and there is a huge difference between "my flesh" and "the flesh"! In the writings of John and Paul, "the flesh" is a phrase usually used to refer to fallen human nature apart from the help of God:

> "You judge according to *the flesh*, I judge no one." (John 8:15, emphasis added)

> While we were living in *the flesh*, our sinful passions, aroused by the law, were at work in our members to bear fruit for death. (Rom 7:5, emphsis added)[8]

By contrast, the flesh of Jesus is salvific! Jesus both *takes on his flesh* in the incarnation and then *gives his flesh* at the crucifixion, the two acts that are pillars of our salvation:

> And the Word became *flesh* and dwelt among us, full of grace and truth. (John 1:14, emphasis added)

> "The bread which I shall give for the life of the world is *my flesh.*" (John 6:51, emphasis added)

No one would take John 6:63 — "the flesh is of no avail" — and use it to argue that the Word becoming flesh (John 1:14) was worthless and pointless. Therefore, they should not use it to argue that the Eucharistic flesh of Jesus in John 6:54 — "he who eats my flesh has eternal life" — is ineffective or insignificant.

---

8   See also John 1:13, 3:6, 17:2; 1 John 2:16; Rom 7:18, 25, 8:3, 5–9, 12–13; 1 Cor 5:5; etc.

I have come to believe that the New Testament Scriptures themselves are completely clear on the point that the Eucharistic bread and wine simply are the flesh of Jesus. That is the plain sense of all the texts in the New Testament that discuss the Eucharist, and Protestants pride themselves on taking the Scriptures in their plain sense. Nonetheless, if it were the case that all the early Christian Fathers explained to the early Church that these apparently obvious texts needed to be taken in a symbolic sense, I would accept it. However, that is precisely what we do *not* find.

Can you imagine a dialogue between an angel and the Apostle John in heaven?

> Angel: "Say John, do you realize the Christians down there think the Eucharistic bread and wine are Jesus' actual body and blood?"
>
> John: "No! Really? That's terrible! Where did they get that idea?"
>
> Angel: "Because you recorded Jesus saying, 'Unless you eat my flesh and drink my blood, you have no life in you.'"
>
> John: "Oh, no! Did I really write that down? I never thought anyone would take that *literally*! What about the part where I explain it's all just a symbol?"
>
> Angel: "You forgot to write that part down."
>
> John: "Well, didn't Luke or Paul explain?"
>
> Angel: "You *all* forgot to write down the part about it being symbolic."

Not only do the New Testament Scriptures identify the Eucharist as Jesus' actual Body and Blood, but the Fathers uniformly and unanimously confirm this. Therefore, I will conclude this chapter with quotes from two of my favorite Fathers.

Irenaeus was the pastor of the Christian community in Lyons, France, in the middle of the A.D. 100s. He is famous for his work *Against Heresies*, which takes to task various schismatic groups who twisted Christian teaching. I read parts of *Against*

Heresies as an undergraduate and in my seminary studies. But I was never exposed to what he said about the Eucharist!

> When, therefore, the mixed cup and the baked bread receives the Word of God and becomes the Eucharist, the Body of Christ, and from these the substance of our flesh is increased and supported, how can they say that the flesh is not capable of receiving the gift of God, which is eternal life — flesh which is nourished by the Body and Blood of the Lord. (*Against Heresies* 5:2:2–3)

Notice that Irenaeus *cannot* have a symbolic understanding of the Eucharist, because if the Eucharist is only a symbol, it never *becomes* anything else. Yet Irenaeus describes it as *becoming* the Body and Blood of the Lord once it *receives* the Word of God — in other words, when the celebrant speaks the words of Jesus at the Last Supper over the bread and wine.

Likewise, Saint Augustine testifies to the Real Presence of Christ in the Eucharist in numerous passages. Saint Augustine was my favorite Father, and many Calvinists consider him the forerunner of Calvin, a sort of proto-Calvin. I read a lot of Augustine as an undergraduate and in seminary — mostly from the *Confessions* and *The City of God*. But again, I was never exposed to what he said about the Eucharist!

> What you see is the bread and the chalice; that is what your own eyes report to you. But what your faith obliges you to accept is that the bread is the Body of Christ and the chalice the Blood of Christ. (*Sermons* 272)

Notice here, too, that Augustine *cannot* have symbolic understanding of the Eucharist, because it takes no faith to believe that something is a symbol. It only takes faith to believe that there has been an unseen transformation of what looks like bread and wine into a different substance. Augustine is asking the early Christians to believe that a miracle has taken place even though their senses cannot perceive it. He has a Catholic understanding of the Eucharist, which later would come to be called *transubstantiation*.

Of course Augustine had such a view. He believed in the plain sense of Scripture — and, now, so do I.

CHAPTER FIVE

Fathers Know Best

Priesthood in the Bible

"Catholics believe that only a few celibate men are priests, whereas we Protestants believe in the 'priesthood of all believers'!" I used to announce triumphantly when catechizing new converts and educating them to be members of my congregation.

In so doing, I was massively misrepresenting Catholic teaching, which I had never actually studied. Many of the "new converts" I worked with were nonpracticing Catholics. Like most Catholics, they had never studied Catholic teaching either. Sometimes it seems like Catholicism is the world's largest, yet least understood, religion.

So, let's set the record straight. The idea of the "priesthood of all believers" is Catholic. Like all true doctrines, the Reformers got this idea from Catholic tradition and from Scripture. We all know the basic Scriptures that teach a priestly status for all Christians. One of the best known is 1 Peter 2:9, in which Peter, speaking to the early Church, declares to them, "You are a chosen race, a *royal priesthood*, a holy nation." Peter asserts here that what God once promised to Israel is now bestowed on the Church. At Sinai, before the covenant was made, God told Moses to declare to the people, "If you will obey my voice and keep my covenant ... you shall be to me a royal *priesthood* and a holy nation."[1]

Of course, Israel did not keep the covenant, but broke it at the Golden Calf incident (Exod 32) and at least ten more times while wandering through the wilderness in the book of Numbers. So, the people of Israel never embraced the promised royal

---

1 Exodus 19:5–7. The phrase in Hebrew translated "royal priesthood" can also be rendered "kingdom of priests." In fact, the New Testament renders it both ways at different times. Compare 1 Peter 2:9 with Revelation 1:6.

priesthood. But the Church does, for all those who receive the sacraments in faith. This is Peter's meaning in 1 Peter 2:9, as well as Paul's teaching in Romans 12:1:

> I appeal to you therefore, brethren, by the mercies of God, to present your bodies as a living sacrifice, holy and acceptable to God, which is your spiritual worship.

It's obvious that Paul employs terms and ideas here from the Israelite priesthood, and that he sees Christian believers taking on a priestly role to offer the sacrifice of their whole lives.

The Church Fathers recognized and taught this. For example, Saint Peter Chrysologus (A.D. 380–450) wrote the following about Romans 12:1:

> Listen now to what the Apostle urges us to do. I appeal to you, he says, to present your bodies as a living sacrifice. By this exhortation of his, *Paul has raised all men to priestly status.* How marvelous is the priesthood of the Christian, for he is both the victim that is offered on his own behalf, and the priest who makes the offering. He does not need to go beyond himself to seek what he is to immolate to God: with himself and in himself he brings the sacrifice he is to offer God for himself. The victim remains and the priest remains, always one and the same. Immolated, the victim still lives: the priest who immolates cannot kill. Truly it is an amazing sacrifice in which a body is offered without being slain and blood is offered without being shed.[2]

All priests, religious brothers and sisters, and many devout lay Catholics are familiar with this teaching of Saint Peter Chrysologus, because it is read in the Divine Office (Liturgy of the Hours) every year on the fourth week of Easter.

Furthermore, the *Catechism of the Catholic Church* explains:

---

2 Saint Peter Chrysologus, Sermon on Peace §108, from the Office of Readings, Tuesday of the Fourth Week of Easter.

The whole Church is a priestly people. Through Baptism all the faithful share in the priesthood of Christ. This participation is called the "common priesthood of the faithful." (CCC 1591)

So, the "priesthood of all believers" is both a Catholic and a scriptural doctrine. How many Catholics really understand it and live it out well? Probably very few. But to be fair, very few Christians in general — whether Protestant, Catholic, or Orthodox — understand and live out this doctrine well. That's a pastoral problem that's beyond the scope of this book (or any book) to solve.[3]

Right now, we are focused on a different issue: granted that all Christians recognize a "common priesthood" of the believer, is there also a further priesthood, a "ministerial priesthood" that exercises leadership in the Church, especially in teaching and sacraments?

Most Protestants deny this, but the Catholic Church affirms it. The *Catechism* teaches:

Based on [the] common priesthood and ordered to its service, there exists another participation in the mission of Christ: the ministry conferred by the sacrament of Holy Orders, where the task is to serve in the name and in the person of Christ the Head in the midst of the community. (CCC 1591)

It's this reality that the Church calls "Holy Orders" or "the ministerial priesthood" that I used to deny, but now affirm — based on Scripture.

Experiences in Ministry

My experiences in actual pastoral ministry prepared me ultimately to accept Catholic teaching on the ministerial priest-

---

3 Various Catholic saints have urged Christians to embrace this common priesthood more fully. Saint Josemaría Escrivá wrote: "All Christians, without exception, have been made priests of our lives, 'to offer spiritual sacrifices acceptable to God through Jesus Christ' (1 Pet 2:5). Everything we do can be an expression of our obedience to God's will and so perpetuate the mission of the God-man" (*Christ Is Passing By*, 96).

hood. As I evangelized, won converts, and began catechizing
new believers, I often ran into the basic rebellious attitude that
characterizes American culture and American Christianity:
"Who the heck are you to tell me what to do?" Even though
people had prayed to receive Jesus into their lives, it didn't necessarily mean that they had a lot of respect for me (or anyone
else) as their pastor. I found myself having to defend my role and
authority from Scripture and became very familiar with those
passages of Scripture that uphold the roles of pastors and other
spiritual leaders, such as Hebrews 13:17:

> Obey your leaders and submit to them; for they are keep-
> ing watch over your souls, as men who will have to give
> account. Let them do this joyfully, and not sadly, for that
> would be of no advantage to you.

It is clear from this passage and others that there *is* an authority
structure in the Church. There are those who lead, and others
who need to follow. Peter also speaks of this:

> So I exhort the elders among you, as a fellow elder [Greek
> *presbuteros*] ... tend the flock of God that is your charge, not
> by constraint but willingly, not for shameful gain but eager-
> ly, not as domineering over those in your charge but being
> examples to the flock.... Likewise you that are younger *be
> subject to the elders [presbuteroi].* (1 Peter 5:1–5, emphasis
> added)[4]

Because of these and other passages, I have never been anti-
authority. A rebellious, anti-authority attitude is not compatible
with true Christianity. Jesus praises the Roman officer who says,
"I am a man under authority" (Matt 8:9, Luke 7:8) and commends
his faith.

Nonetheless, I have run into Protestants who believe in total
egalitarianism and claim that pastors are "unbiblical." I don't know
how they can believe that, since pastors are mentioned in Eph 4:11
and elsewhere. Furthermore, it is often the case that these "egalitar-

---

4   This passage is significant because, among other things, Peter
uses the term *presbuteros*, "elder," which eventually became the English
word "priest."

ian" Christian sects are seriously hierarchical or even tyrannical in practice, with certain "more equal" members controlling the others in a spiritual version of George Orwell's *Animal Farm*.

That was not my attitude. When I moved to Notre Dame in 1999, I knew that Christ's church needed a spiritual hierarchy and pastors. I wasn't opposed to ordained clergy. But I objected to calling clergy "priest" and "father," and I didn't see any continuity between the Old Testament priesthood and the leaders of the New Testament church. Those are the issues I want to tackle in the rest of this chapter.

Confusion of Terms

Before we go any further, we need to lay out a basic confusion in terminology that plagues English-speaking Christians. The issue is the history of the word "priest." In the Old Testament, the Hebrew word for the Israelite priests is *kohen* (plural *kohanim*), which became Greek *hierus* (plural *hiereis*) when the Scriptures were translated into the Greek Septuagint in 250 B.C.

In the New Testament, the leaders of the Church are not called *hiereis*, but rather *episkopoi* (literally, "overseers" or "supervisors") and *presbuteroi* (literally, "elders"). The Greek words *episkopoi* and *presbuteroi* became corrupted over time and eventually entered the English language through German (*bischof* and *priester*), giving us the words "bishop" and "priest" respectively.

Later, when the Old Testament was translated into English, the translators used "priest" to render the Hebrew *kohen* (Greek *hiereus*). So, we have an odd situation where a derivative of the Greek word for "elder" came to translate the Greek word for "priest." We are stuck with this situation, however, because there is no other English word for the concept of a religious leader invested with sacred authority except *priest*.

As a result, most English translations render *episkopoi* and *presbuteroi* in the New Testament more literally as "overseer" and "elder" respectively. This choice in translation prevents the English reader from seeing the organic connection between these roles and the "bishops" and "priests" who serve in the Catholic Church to this day. So, many English-speaking Christians will say, "Priests are never mentioned in the New Testament! Priesthood is an Old

Testament concept!" A lot of this is just due to language confusion. Something was definitely lost in translation!

Continuity between the Old Testament Priesthood and the New Testament Priesthood

Nonetheless, there are numerous indications in the New Testament that the duties and roles of the Old Testament priesthood were reassigned by Jesus to his apostles and that they, in turn, bestowed that responsibility on others.

For example, many scholars have seen that Jesus claims the rights and privileges of the priesthood for himself and his disciples in the incident recorded in Matthew 12:

> At that time Jesus went through the grainfields on the Sabbath; his disciples were hungry, and they began to pluck heads of grain and to eat. But when the Pharisees saw it, they said to him, "Look, your disciples are doing what is not lawful to do on the Sabbath." He said to them, "Have you not read what David did, when he was hungry, and those who were with him: how he entered the house of God and ate the bread of the Presence, which it was not lawful for him to eat nor for those who were with him, but only for the priests? Or have you not read in the law how on the Sabbath the priests in the temple profane the Sabbath, and are guiltless? I tell you, something greater than the temple is here." (Matt 12:1–6)

Notice that Jesus defends his apostles by citing two priestly examples: (1) an incident in which David and his men exercised the priestly privilege of consuming the bread of the Presence (1 Sam 21:1–6); and (2) the example of the Levitical priests serving in the Temple. The famous American rabbi, Jacob Neusner — one of the most prolific Jewish Bible scholars of the twentieth century — draws the obvious implications from this passage when read through Jewish eyes: "He [Jesus] and his disciples may do on the Sabbath what they do because they stand in the place of the priests in the Temple."[5]

---

5 Quoted by Pope Benedict XVI, *Jesus of Nazareth*, Vol. 1, 108.

The Old Testament priests had responsibility for (1) offering sacrifice, (2) mediating the forgiveness of sin, (3) interpreting the law, and (4) serving in the Temple. In the pages of the Gospels, we see all these roles being given to the apostles.

Offering Sacrifice

Jesus authorizes the apostles to offer sacrifice when he shows them how to offer his own body and blood and then commands them, "Do this in *remembrance* of me." Body is separated from blood only when an animal or human dies. Therefore, the separate offering of Jesus' body and blood at the Last Supper implies his death. In the priesthood, one was trained to separate body from blood and offer the slain animals as sacrifice, as we see in Leviticus 1–7.

Furthermore, the command "Do this in *remembrance*" has a liturgical, sacrificial connotation to it that is lost on modern readers, who forget that there was a "remembrance" or "memorial" offering in the Old Testament ritual for worship (Lev 2:2, 9, 16, 5:12, 6:15; Num 5:26). Even the humble word "do" in the phrase "Do this in remembrance of me" has special force. In Greek, it is *poieo*, "to do, make, perform," and it is used frequently in the Old Testament in priestly contexts with the sense "perform a sacrifice." For examples see Lev 4:20, 5:10, 6:15, 14:19, 15:15, 30, 16:24; Num 6:11, 16.

The Old Testament included a "thanksgiving" (Hebrew *todah*) sacrifice (see Lev 7:11–15), mentioned frequently in the Psalms (e.g., Ps 50:14, 23, 56:12, 100:1, 107:22, 116:17). The ancient rabbis said that when the Messiah came, only the thanksgiving or *todah* sacrifice would still be performed, since there would no longer be need of atonement, but only of thanksgiving for the salvation brought by the Messiah.[6] "Thanksgiving" in Greek is *eucharistia*. The Eucharist is the new thanksgiving or *todah* sacrifice, which Jesus commanded his priest-apostles to perform until he returned.

---

6   Hartmut Gese, *Essays On Biblical Theology* (Minneapolis: Augsburg Publishing House, 1981), 133.

Forgiveness of Sins

Jesus authorizes his disciples to mediate the forgiveness of sins when "he breathed on them and said to them, 'Receive the Holy Spirit. Whose sins you forgive are forgiven them; whose sins you retain are retained" (John 20:23). As we have seen in chapter three, on confession, it was the priests who were responsible for mediating the forgiveness of sins in the Old Testament (Lev 4:20, 26, 31, 35, 5:10, 13, 16, 18, 6:7, 19:22; Num 15:25, 28).

Interpreting the Law

Jesus authorizes his disciples to interpret the law when he says, "Whatever you bind on earth will be bound in heaven, whatever you loose on earth will be loosed in heaven" (Matt 16:18, 18:18).

We spoke of this in chapter one and pointed out how "bind and loose" referred to the *halakhic* authority to interpret the law for daily living. In Jesus' own day, this authority was exercised among the Jews by the scribes and Pharisees. However, this was not always the case. The rise of the scribes and Pharisees did not occur until the Maccabean period (c. 165–66 B.C.). It was in this period that we start to get Jewish "rabbis," that is, teachers who arose to teach people the law, because the priesthood had become corrupt.

Earlier in Israel's history, it was the priests who had responsibility for teaching and interpreting the law. This is clear from numerous passages,[7] especially Deut 17:8–13, where difficult questions of the interpretation of the law are handed over to the Levitical priests, and Hag 2:10–14, where the prophet instructs the people to go ask the priests how to interpret the law of cleanliness. Again, the only reason why the scribes and Pharisees were doing this in Jesus' day was because under the Maccabees in the 100s B.C., the high priests with the proper bloodline were deposed and replaced by men without legitimate ancestry, and chief priestly roles were doled out for political reasons. Thus, the priesthood could no longer be trusted.

---

7 Num 31:21; Deut 17:18, 31:9, 33:10; 2 Kings 17:27; 2 Chr 15:3; Ezra 7:12, 21; Neh 8:2, 9; Jer 2:8, 18:18; Ezek 7:26, 22:26, 44:23; Zeph 3:4; Mal 2:1–9.

Serving in the Temple

Finally, Jesus authorizes the apostles to serve in the sanctuary. We see this in John 14:2–3:

> "In my Father's house are many rooms; if it were not so, would I have told you that I go to prepare a place for you? And when I go and prepare a place for you, I will come again and will take you to myself, that where I am you may be also."

Modern readers don't hear the Temple themes in this passage, but in Israelite culture, the term "place" (Hebrew *maqom*, Greek *topos*) usually meant "sacred place" and specifically the Temple, as we see in John 11:48, where the priests refer to the Temple as their "place" (Greek *topos*). This is confirmed by the phrase "my Father's house," which Jesus uses to refer to the Temple (see Luke 2:49), and the idea of "many rooms," since the Temple was the largest building in the whole nation and filled with an abundance of storage chambers. Jesus is preparing a "temple" for his new "priests" to serve in. In one sense, this temple is the Church, as we see from the Temple imagery applied to the Church in Ephesians 2:19–22.

Actually, this Temple image in John 14 fits into a larger pattern of priestly imagery that runs through the whole Last Supper discourse in John 13–17, the longest teaching of Jesus in the Gospels. This discourse begins with priestly imagery in the foot-washing episode of John 13 and ends with priestly imagery in the so-called "High Priestly Prayer" of John 17. Let's look at both these passages briefly.

Footwashing and Priesthood: The footwashing episode in John 13 is full of motifs from the Day of Atonement and priestly ordination rituals. The Day of Atonement (Yom Kippur) was the holiest day of the Jewish calendar, when the High Priest entered the Holy of Holies of the Jerusalem Temple and made atonement for all the people. Theologian Leroy Huizenga, himself a convert from Protestantism, notes the following:

In John 13 we find parallels to Leviticus 16, the Day of Atonement ritual. Leviticus 16:23–24 reads, "Then Aaron shall come into the tent of meeting, and shall put off the linen garments which he put on when he went into the holy place, and shall leave them there; and he shall bathe his body in water in a holy place, and put on his garments, and come forth, and offer his burnt offering and the burnt offering of the people, and make atonement for himself and for the people." Observe the pattern: The high priest undresses, bathes, dresses, and offers sacrifice. In John 13, Jesus undresses (v. 4), washes the disciples' feet (v. 5–11), dresses (v. 12), and will soon offer himself in sacrifice. Whereas in Leviticus the high priest washes all of himself, in John, Jesus washes the feet of the disciples. Jesus is sharing his high priesthood with the disciples; he must wash them — ordain them as priests — lest they have "no part" in his priesthood.[8]

The washing of feet also connotes the role of the priesthood, because the priests had to wash their feet to perform any ministry in the sanctuary (Exod 30:19–21). Prior to this, at their ordination, they had a full bath (Lev 8:6). We see Peter and Jesus discussing the full bath versus the washing of the feet in John 13:6–10. In that same passage, Jesus insists Peter must submit to the washing in order to have a "part" (Greek *meris*) in Jesus. This word *meris* is used several times in the Pentateuch to refer to the fact that the Levitical priests have no "part" in the land because their "part" is God alone (Num 18:20; Deut 10:9, 12:12, 14:27, 29; Josh 18:7). The analogy is clear: Peter is being prepared for a new kind of priesthood wherein his "part" is going to be God alone, that is to say, Jesus alone.

High Priestly Prayer and Priesthood: Jesus' prayer in John 17 is also full of Day of Atonement and priesthood motifs. We read in Leviticus 16:17 that the Day of Atonement ritual consisted of

---

8 Leroy Huizenga, "Holy Thursday, Footwashing, and the Institution of the Priesthood," *The Catholic World Report*, http://www.catholicworldreport.com/2014/04/16/holy-thursday-footwashing-and-the-institution-of-the-priesthood/.

three parts: atonement for the High Priest himself, for his house (i.e., the rest of the priests), and for the entire people. We find that John 17 is structured the same way: first Jesus prays for himself (vv. 1–5), then the apostles (i.e., the rest of the priests; vv. 6–19), and then for the entire church (vv. 20–26).

Furthermore, in Jesus' time the Day of Atonement ritual was marked by the pronunciation of the divine name. It was the only day on which the Divine Name (YHWH) was actually pronounced, when the High Priest would bless the people after the atonement ritual.[9] Look through John 17, and you will find many references to Jesus "making known" the Father's Name (17:6, 12, 26).

Finally, Jesus speaks of "consecrating" or "sanctifying" the apostles in John 17:17–19. This is the Greek word *hagiazo*, which is applied to male human beings in the Old Testament almost exclusively in the context of priestly ordination.[10] The sense is that the apostles are being "ordained" to serve as priests of the New Testament.

Thus, the beginning and end of the Last Supper Discourse in John is marked by themes of the Day of Atonement and of priestly ordination and service. Then, Jesus and the apostles leave the Upper Room and the Passion ensues. When they reconvene in the Upper Room after the Resurrection in John 20:19–23, Jesus completes their "ordination" by bestowing on them the Holy Spirit, which will empower them to perform the priestly role of the mediation of forgiveness of sins.

Thus, a wealth of Gospel texts indicate that the apostles take over the roles of the Old Testament priests and become a priesthood of the New Testament.

Nothing Succeeds like Succession

Now, many readers will follow me this far and be willing to concede that the apostles constituted a kind of priesthood. However, they will balk — as I did — at the idea that this priesthood was passed on to successors. But the idea that all the roles of the New

9 Mishna Yoma 3:8, 4:2.

10 See Exod 19:22, 28:41, 29:1, 33, 44, 30:30, 40:13; Lev 8:11–12, 21:8.

Testament priesthood ceased with the apostles doesn't make sense. We have to believe that Jesus Our Lord knew his Church was going to last for many, many generations. Wouldn't there be a need for those authorized to forgive sin, interpret the law, offer sacrifice, and so on, throughout the life of the Church, and not just for the first thirty years?

In any event, as we have seen briefly already, the New Testament itself shows the apostles designating other men with a measure of their authority in order to continue their ministry when they could not be physically present. We see the apostles appointing the first deacons in Acts 6:1–7. The apostles also appointed "elders" or *presbuteroi* in all the Churches (Acts 14:23). At the first church council in Acts 15, we see that these *presbuteroi* shared in the governance of the church along with the apostles (see esp. vv. 6, 22, 23, 16:4). The decision reached by the first church council is described as coming from the authority of the "apostles and [*presbuteroi*]" (Acts 15:23), so the apostles must have entrusted some of their authority to these men.

In 1 Timothy 4:14, we see the beginnings of ordination as Paul refers to the council of *presbuteroi* who "laid hands" on Timothy. These *presbuteroi* are to "rule ... teach and preach" (1 Tim 5:17), which were tasks that the apostles originally performed in Acts 1–15. Paul's disciple Titus appears to bear the status of a *presbuteros* or an *episkopos*, and Paul authorizes him to appoint more *presbuteroi* for the churches in Titus 1:5: "The reason I left you in Crete ... [was to] appoint [*presbuteroi*] in every town." This passage is *extremely* important, because it shows us that the duty to appoint *presbuteroi*, which originally was the role of the apostles themselves (Acts 16:4), is now delegated to a disciple or representative of the apostles (Titus 1:5).

Peter stresses that the *presbuteroi* share in the apostolic ministry to shepherd (pastor) the people of God (1 Peter 5:5). Peter stresses the close connection between the *presbuteroi* and the apostles by identifying himself — the chief apostle — as a *presbuteros*:

> So I exhort the [*presbuteroi*] among you, as a fellow [*presbuteros*] and a witness of the sufferings of Christ as well as a

partaker in the glory that is to be revealed. Tend the flock of God that is your charge. (1 Pet 5:1)

This passage needs also to be read against the triple commissioning of Peter as the chief "shepherd" or "pastor" of Jesus' flock in John 21. We see that Peter regards the *presbuteroi* as sharing with him his responsibility to shepherd or pastor the people of God. In time, the Church would use the term "successor," and speak of the "successors" of the apostles.

When we move from the New Testament into the writings of the early Fathers, we see continuity of this thought. Clement of Rome, who was probably ordained by Peter,[11] writes the following in his famous letter *1 Clement*, writing about twenty years after Peter penned his first letter:

> Our apostles likewise knew, through our Lord Jesus Christ, that there would be strife over the bishop's office. For this reason, therefore, having received complete foreknowledge, they appointed the officials mentioned earlier and afterwards they gave the offices a permanent character; that is, if they should die, other approved men should succeed to their ministry. Those, therefore, who were appointed by them or, later on, by other reputable men with the consent of the whole Church, and who have ministered to the flock of Christ blamelessly, humbly, peaceably, and unselfishly, and for a long time have been well-spoken of by all — these men we consider to be unjustly removed from their ministry. For it will be no small sin for us, if we depose from the bishop's office those who have offered the gifts blamelessly and in holiness. Blessed are those presbyters who have gone on ahead, who took their departure at a mature and fruitful age, for they need

---

11   Irenaeus, writing c. A.D. 180, says, "Clement was allotted the bishopric. This man, as he had seen the blessed apostles, and had been conversant with them, might be said to have the preaching of the apostles still echoing [in his ears], and their traditions before his eyes" (*Against Heresies* 3.3.3).

no longer fear that someone might remove them from their established place. (1 Clem 44:1–5)

We see here how Clement doesn't make a very clear distinction between *episkopos* (bishop) and *presbuteros* (priest); he treats them as almost synonymous. By the time of Ignatius of Antioch, some twenty years later, however, the Church had adopted the practice of reserving the term *episkopos* (supervisor) for the chief *presbuteros* in a metropolitan area, whereas the rest of the clergy retained the title *presbuteroi*.[12] That is the practice that has continued to this day.

The point of what we are saying is this: the New Testament is clear, when read through Jewish eyes, that the apostles are taking over the roles of the Old Testament priesthood.

The New Testament is also clear that, within their own lifetimes, the apostles appointed other men, called *presbuteroi* or *episkopoi*, who shared with them in the governance and the shepherding/pastoring of the Church — in other words, shared with them in the priestly responsibilities.

We even see men appointed by the apostles *themselves appointing others* to share in this ministry (Titus 1:5). This is the principle of succession — and the writings of the early Fathers who knew the apostles (i.e., Clement and Ignatius) describe this process continuing. So, the apostles were the fountainhead of the New Testament priesthood, and this priesthood was transmitted to the *episkopoi* and *presbuteroi* who succeeded them, down to the bishops and priests of today.

Therefore, Saint Augustine writes:

12 Ignatius of Antioch writes to the Smyrnean Christians the following around A.D. 106: "You must all follow the bishop, as Jesus Christ followed the Father, and follow the presbytery [i.e., the body of presbyters] as you would the apostles;… It is not permissible either to baptize or to hold a love feast without the bishop. But whatever he approves is also pleasing to God" (Smyrneans 8:1–2). Note that when he says, "Whatever [the bishop] approves is also pleasing to God," Ignatius is reflecting the concept of the bishop as successor of the apostles, to whom Jesus said, "What you loose on earth will be loosed in heaven" (Mt 18:18).

There are many other things which most properly can keep me in [the Catholic Church's] bosom.... The *succession of priests*, from the very seat of the apostle Peter, to whom the Lord, after his resurrection, gave the charge of feeding his sheep [John 21:15–17], up to the present *episcopate*, keeps me here.[13]

Protestant Succession

Maybe this is a good place for me to mention a certain inconsistency that I noticed for a long time when I was a Protestant. As a seminarian, I trained for four years in the seminary with the expectation that when I graduated my denomination would *ordain* me as a pastor. The ordination ceremony marked the beginning of my career. Without ordination, I couldn't serve as a pastor in my denomination or exercise any kind of authority within it.

The ordination ceremony consisted of older elders and pastors laying their hands on me and praying for me, that the Holy Spirit would empower me for the ministry of the pastorate. The word "ordain," which we used, comes ultimately from the Latin *ordo*, "to put in order," from which the name "Holy Orders" also comes. It had to be performed by men who were already ordained. They, in turn, had been ordained by the previous generation of clergy, and so on, back to the beginning of our denomination. So, you can see that we, even as Protestants, recognized in practice the principle of succession. You could not be a pastor in our denomination unless you were recognized and approved by the previous generation of pastors.

Of course, you can see the ultimate problem. This Protestant succession only works back as far as the beginning of our denomination. That's where things got murky. Who ordained the founders? Who authorized them to start a new church? I knew that my tradition — if not my individual denomination — traced back to John Calvin. But it's not clear that John Calvin was ever ordained by anyone. Who put him in charge? Who had the authority to get this ball rolling?

---

13 *Against the Letter of Mani Called "The Foundation"* 4:5 [A.D. 397].

The point is this: Protestants recognize the principle that the new generation of church leadership needs to be approved by the previous generation. That is a form of succession. Yet we had no coherent explanation for the *beginning* of the succession in our denomination. There was no way to explain it, because our succession did not go back in an unbroken chain to the apostles like Catholic succession does. At one or more points in our history, there was a disruption in which unauthorized persons started a new church and placed themselves at the head of it. But that kind of maverick behavior by Christians is never endorsed in Scripture.

Some might cite Saint Paul as an example of "doing one's own thing" without authorization from anyone (Gal 1:16–17), but Saint Paul could claim a direct apparition from Jesus and could perform miracles (Acts 13:11–12). Even with direct authorization from Jesus (Gal 1:12), he still went to Jerusalem to establish communion with Peter (Gal 1:18–19), then later sought the approval of his doctrine from the original body of apostles (Gal 2:2, 9), and received the laying on of hands from the *presbuteroi* of the church in Antioch (Acts 13:3). Paul kept communion with the other leaders of the Church.

So, even as a Protestant seminarian and acting pastor, I was bothered by this inconsistency in our Church government — that we acknowledged the principle of succession except when it came to our own origins. Further, I was bothered by the fact that the New Testament never gave instructions about how or when to start one's own church, or under what conditions one should break away from an existing Church. The New Testament did not see that as a possibility or necessity. Instead, we find exhortations like this:

> Obey your leaders and submit to them; for they are keeping watch over your souls, as men who will have to give account. (Heb 13:17)

But if every Christian is free to rise up and start a new denomination, it truly renders meaningless the command to "obey and submit" to one's leaders. Hebrews does not say, "Obey your leaders unless you think they are really bad, and then go start your own church." But that's what actually has happened and continues to happen in Protestant traditions.

But what happens if you have a leader who is corrupt? Obviously, that does pose a problem. Within the Catholic Church, there is a basic system of appeal to handle this. One can appeal above the local priest to the bishop, and above the bishop to the successor of Peter, the Pope. The final judgment of the bishop of Rome (the Pope) must be trusted, even if it seems to be hard to accept at the moment, because the bishop of Rome is the heir to the promise, "What you bind on earth will be bound in heaven." This is the only way to maintain the unity of the Church. All other systems perpetuate schisms and the proliferation of new, independent churches that, in time, show all the same weaknesses of their parent churches.

The Mystery of Church Government

I remember my church government professor in seminary remarking once that it seemed odd that the Scriptures were not clearer on how the Church was to be governed. Years later, I asked an older relative of mine who is a Protestant pastor what form of church government the New Testament actually taught. He told me frankly, "I don't know." Another professor remarked that church government tended to imitate the political structures of any given society. In my tradition, we regarded the government of the church and the arrangement of her leadership as something the Scriptures did not define, and each denomination was free to do as it wished.

Why would Jesus remain silent about so obvious a question as the government of the Church he established (Matt 16:18)? Actually, neither Jesus nor the New Testament *are* silent on the government of the Church; it's just that as Protestants we could not accept the principles they teach. So, we were just "blind" to them.

However, what in fact we see in the New Testament is Jesus appointing the Twelve (Mark 3:14) who in turn appoint others (Acts 1:15–26, 6:3, 13:3, 14:23), who in turn appoint others (Titus 1:5). The New Testament does not foresee a failure of this system. The New Testament assumes that its readers still have legitimate leaders to whom they owe obedience and submission (Heb 13:17). Nowhere does it instruct or encourage the creation of new churches that are not in communion with older churches.

The issues that we have discussed in this chapter are not private issues of concern just for Catholics, or for Catholic-Protestant polemics. The issues raised in this chapter are of universal concern for all who claim to follow Jesus. Did Jesus really desire a diverse group of independent denominations? John 17 indicates otherwise. If not, then how did Jesus intend his church to be governed and its unity maintained? I have presented strong scriptural evidence, backed up by the testimony of the early church pastors (Fathers), that Jesus and the apostles established a self-perpetuating succession of leaders, called *episkopoi* and *presbuteroi*, who would carry on the work of leadership of the church after the lives of the first apostles. All Christians need to grapple with these texts and ask themselves whether they are willing to embrace them, or are in the practice rejecting them by explaining them away.

Epilogue: Calling Priests "Father"

There's one last issue that we need to deal with, and that is the practice of calling priests "Father." As a Protestant, I objected to this practice on what I thought was extremely strong scriptural grounds. Jesus says to call "no man on earth 'father'":

> "But you are not to be called rabbi, for you have one teacher, and you are all brethren. And call no man your father on earth, for you have one Father, who is in heaven. Neither be called masters, for you have one master, the Christ. He who is greatest among you shall be your servant; whoever exalts himself will be humbled, and whoever humbles himself will be exalted." (Matt 23:8–12)

On the face of it, it seems pretty simple, right? Jesus says don't call anyone on earth "father," so we shouldn't call priests "father."

But then things get more complicated — because we all have human fathers that we do call "father," "papa," "pa," "dad," and all sorts of other synonyms. So, all Protestants violate the clear teaching of Matthew 23:9 by referring to their own dads as "father."

"But no!" comes the response, "Jesus is only talking about calling men 'father' *in a religious sense.*" Really? It doesn't say that in Matthew. The verse says "call no man your father on earth," not, "call no man your father on earth *in a religious sense.*" Therefore, anyone who calls their dad "Father" is either violating the teaching of Jesus, or else admitting that the Bible needs to be interpreted beyond its plain sense. I think the second option is correct: the Bible, including the words of Jesus, sometimes has to be interpreted beyond its plain sense.

As a matter of fact, there are many instances in the New Testament where Jesus or one of the apostles calls a human being "father," apparently without committing a sin. When telling the parable of the rich man and Lazarus, Jesus refers to Israel's patriarch as "Father Abraham" (Luke 16:24).[14] Likewise, Saint Paul calls Abraham "father" in several passages (Rom 4:11), even referring to him as "the father of us all" (4:16). Paul goes on to liken himself to a father (Phil 2:22; 1 Th 2:11), and he boldly tells the Corinthians "I have become your father in Christ Jesus through the Gospel," and speaks of Onesimus, "whose father I became in prison" (Phil 1:10). Elsewhere, he unashamedly refers to the "fathers" of Israel (1 Cor 10:11, Gal 1:14).

Then there is the striking statement of the apostle John, who, when writing to an unidentified congregation in 1 John, says:

> I am writing to you, *fathers*, because you know him who is from the beginning. I am writing to you, young men, because you have overcome the evil one. I write to you, children, because you know the Father. (1 John 2:13, emphasis added)

This passage is very interesting because it identifies three categories of believers in the congregation: the fathers, the young men, and the children. Most commentators do not believe that John means these categories in a literal sense, i.e., males from age one

---

14 "And he called out, 'Father Abraham, have mercy upon me.'" (Luke 16:24).

to twelve, males from thirteen to twenty-five, and then males who have children.

Even Protestant commentators acknowledge that John probably is referring to different categories of spiritual maturity: "children" might be catechumens, "young men" those initiated into the faith, and "fathers" as the leaders the congregation, whom we know from other texts were usually called the *presbuteroi*, "elders."[15] If this interpretation is correct, however, then 1 John 2:13 is the first recorded instance of Christian *presbuteroi*, priests, being called "fathers!" This practice, then, has scriptural precedent.

So, then, let us recap. In Matthew 23:9, Jesus says not to call anyone "father," but we find the apostles calling themselves and other persons "father" in numerous places in inspired Scripture.[16] Are the apostles violating the teachings of Jesus Himself? Of course not. They just recognize that Jesus was not speaking literally in Matthew 23:8–12.

So, then, what does Jesus mean when he says, "Call no man on earth your 'father'?"

The background for this statement goes back to the meaning of the *name* in Hebrew thought. The *name* of something, in Israelite literature, was its essence or *nature*.

Let's give some classic examples from the Old Testament. At the burning bush, Moses asks for God's name, and God responds: "I AM WHO I AM" (Exod 3:14). However, the phrase "I AM WHO I AM" is *never once* used as the name of God elsewhere in the Bible or by any Israelite writer. It is not a "name" in our sense of the term; rather, it is a description of God's essence.

Later, after the golden calf incident, God "proclaimed the name of the Lord" (Exod 33:19) in the following words:

---

15 See Glen W. Barker, "1 John," *The Expositor's Bible Commentary*, vol. 12, Frank E. Gaebelein, ed. (Grand Rapids, MI: Zondervan, 1981), 320.

16 For that matter, Jesus and the apostles also violate the prohibition on the terms "master" and "teacher" as well. See John 3:10; Acts 5:34, 13:1; 1 Cor 12:28; Eph 4:11; 1 Tim 2:7; 2 Tim 1:11; Heb 5:12; James 3:1; Eph 6:5, 9; Col 3:22, 4:1; 1 Tim 6:1–2; 2 Tim 2:21; Tit 1:8, 2:9; 1 Pet 2:18.

"The LORD, the LORD, a God merciful and gracious, slow to anger, and abounding in steadfast love and faithfulness, keeping steadfast love for thousands, forgiving iniquity and transgression and sin, but who will by no means clear the guilty, visiting the iniquity of the fathers upon the children and the children's children, to the third and the fourth generation." (Exod 34:6–7)

But this long paragraph is nowhere employed as a "name" for God elsewhere in Scripture. It is not a "name" in our sense, but a description of God's *essence* or *nature*.

Again, in a famous passage immortalized by the sublime twelfth chorus of Handel's *Messiah*, the prophet Isaiah says of the coming Son of David:

And his name shall be called, "Wonderful counselor, the mighty God, the everlasting Father, the Prince of Peace."

But look into it: in no passage of the New Testament is Jesus ever called any of these titles as a "name." So, was Isaiah's prophecy unfulfilled? (This used to bother me, actually, when I was a kid, just learning to read Scripture.) But the answer is no. Isaiah's prophecy was not unfulfilled. What the prophet meant by "his name shall be called" is "his essence shall be."

This Hebrew "name" idiom must be taken as the background for Matthew 23:8–12 and the triple prohibition of the "names" master, father, and teacher. In literal fact, Christians (and Jesus himself!) have violated this "prohibition" by calling people master, father, and teacher down through the ages. That is because Christians have understood — if not consciously, at least in their hearts — that Jesus was speaking according to an ancient Hebrew idiom, meaning that we should recognize that no one on earth is *essentially* our master, father, or teacher. Human beings have those roles in our lives *only in a relative sense.* For the sake of good order in the Church and in society, we recognize those who hold those authority roles: in fact, Scripture requires that we recognize their authority. However, at the same time, we know that in an ultimate sense, there is only one Father, Teacher, and Master before whom each one of us will stand on the day of judgment.

When Catholics — and other Christians, for that matter — do not take the prohibitions of Matthew 23:18–22 in a literal sense, they are not doing it out of convenience, as if to say, "We follow Jesus' easy commands literally, but the hard ones we interpret figuratively." Not at all! Rather, we are following a coherent principle: *the example of the apostles.* Whenever there is a question of whether or not to interpret Jesus literally or figuratively, our first question should be, "How did the apostles understand him?" As we have seen with the case of "calling no man father," the apostles obviously *did not* understand Jesus to be speaking literally, because they proceeded to call people "father" in all kinds of senses and contexts in the Scriptures I mentioned above.

On the other hand, when Jesus says, "This is my Body," we do not find the apostles taking it in a figurative sense. On the contrary, Saint Paul warns that unworthy communion in the Lord's Supper is a profanation of the very Body and Blood of the Lord, and that it may result in death (1 Cor 11:27–30). It would be quite different if Saint Paul had explained that the Eucharist was just a symbol — just as he explains that idols aren't really anything and therefore food symbolically offered to them is still fine for consumption (1 Cor 8:1–10, 10:19). But he never does; nor does any other apostle.

So, let me repeat: the principle is *apostolic example.* The example of the apostles shows us that Jesus spoke in Matthew 23:8–12 according to the classic Hebrew idiom of the "name" meaning the "essence." Saint John himself witnesses to the early practice of calling the *presbuteroi* of the congregation "fathers" (1 John 2:13), and Christians have been continuing this practice ever since.

CHAPTER SIX

The Bible Alone Leaves Me Lonely

I mentioned in previous chapters how actually working as a Protestant pastor and evangelist weakened my faith in the rallying cry of the Reformation, "*Sola scriptura!*" or "*The Bible alone!*"

Of course, what the Protestant reformers meant by this phrase has to be unpacked, because they didn't mean that the Bible alone is all that is needed for salvation, apart from faith, God's grace, the preaching of the Gospel, and many other things. No, indeed! The "Bible alone" really means "the Bible interpreted without the help of tradition or the Church." For most of Christian history — and still today in Catholic and Orthodox churches — the Christian tradition and the decisions of the Church were considered a *help* to understanding the Bible. For the Protestant reformers, the tradition and the Church began to be seen more and more as a *hindrance* to understanding Scripture, and the Bible needed to be "freed" from the corrupting influence of centuries of interpretation within the Church. So *sola scriptura* meant, in effect, the Bible without the Church.

When I was a Protestant pastor, however, I would probably have not explained the doctrine of *sola scriptura* so starkly. I would have said "the Bible alone" means that all that is necessary for salvation and the full and complete living of the Christian life are contained in the Bible, without any need for statements of the Church or writings of the Fathers. There was a little bit of irony in this attitude, because in actual fact, in order to be a pastor in my denomination, I had to formally commit myself not only to the Bible, but also to three historic doctrinal statements from various synods of Calvinist churches from the early period of the Reformation. Ironically, these church doctrinal statements taught that Scripture alone was all that was necessary, apart from statements by the Church!

The Calvinist tradition — and Protestantism generally — did not and does not always pit the Bible and the Church's tradition in adversarial roles against each other. On certain issues, the Church Fathers or different historic creeds were accepted as true and helpful in explaining the meaning of Scripture. But Scripture itself finally stood above the interpretive authority of the tradition or the Church.

At first, that sounds good and holy. "The Word of God stands above any human authority!" "Amen, brother!" We can shout that and slap each other on the back and feel like we are being very righteous, upholding the honor and majesty of God. But this concept meant that in theory, or even in practice, any given Church council, father, theologian, or pope could be wrong. Theoretically, the entire Church could have misunderstood a certain Scripture for two thousand years, until some individual Christian came along and understood it properly for the first time. That, in turn, meant that one could never be certain that Christians had properly understood Scripture. Therefore, any and every doctrine could potentially be called into question, and nothing was ever really settled.

Every Christian, moreover, was potentially their own "pope," and could decide for themselves what Scripture meant. You can see that this kind of thinking leads to the dissolving of the Church down to each individual Christian with his own Bible. That has happened. For example, it is said of Roger Williams, the renegade Protestant pastor who founded the state of Rhode Island, that at the end of his life he would celebrate the Lord's Supper by himself because he wasn't confident that even his wife held to correct doctrine. That's pretty lonely. The "Bible alone" left Williams lonely, as it does us all, because it isolates each one of us as our ultimate interpreter of God's Word.

Such complete individualism is not practical, of course, and Christians tend to band together in like-minded groups called denominations. The denomination that I belonged to, for example, had bonded together around three doctrinal statements from Calvinist synods from the early Reformation period, plus a number of other informal statements and commitments, such as the support of independent Christian day schools and the rejection of membership in the Masons or other secret societies.

Our denomination held a synod every year, and the synod had complete power, in principle, to change any aspect of church law or doctrine. As a result, the church government manual had to be updated annually. Potentially, anything and everything could be changed every year. In practice, only currently trending issues were on the table for potential change. So, year after year, the synod would slowly adapt the teaching of our church to be more in line with American culture. This was easy to observe, and very frustrating for those of us who believed that truth was truth, and didn't need to be revised on an annual basis.

But I digress. Let me return to the story of how I lost faith in the "Bible alone," but found greater faith in the Word of God. I entered seminary as a very ardent and eager young Calvinist in the early 1990s. I was convinced of the truth of the "Reformed faith" (Calvinists whose roots go back to continental Europe often identify themselves as "Reformed" Christians). However, when I began my seminary courses, I quickly noticed that my professors spoke not of the "Reformed faith" but of the "Reformed tradition." They would say things like, "In the Reformed tradition, we understand predestination in this way." Or, "In the Reformed tradition, the church is governed without bishops." This immediately rubbed me the wrong way. "Stop talking about the Reformed tradition," I thought to myself, "as Reformed, we are *against* tradition! We stand for the one unchanging Gospel, expressed in the Reformed faith!"

Eventually, I brought up my concerns to one of my professors who was a family friend. "Why are we always talking about the Reformed tradition rather than the Reformed faith?" I asked. He gently explained that there was no denying we were part of a tradition. All Christians were part of some tradition, whether they recognized it or not. There was a Baptist tradition, a Lutheran tradition, a Catholic tradition, an Eastern Orthodox tradition, and a Reformed tradition. Since we were in this last category, he insisted, we should try to be faithful to that tradition.

Well, this bothered me quite a bit. It suggested that each Christian should embrace whatever tradition he or she was born into, whether it was right or wrong. I didn't want to be Reformed simply because I was born into it. I believed being Reformed was *right*, and that all Christians should be Reformed. I soon found, however, that many of my professors, even ones I admired, did not see things this way. This lead to a series of disillusioning encounters with men I respected and looked up to as models.

Since my wife and I had our first child very early in my seminary career, I had to find work to support us, and that meant taking on the role of acting pastor at the small inner-city mission that I've mentioned before. Working in this small neighborhood of a few thousand people in the heart of Michigan's second city, I ran into many other pastors from other Christian traditions: Baptist, Charismatic, Pentecostal, liberal Calvinist, Apostolic, and others. Since my little church was so small, it was not possible for me to live in a Reformed "bubble," like some of my fellow pastors who lived in townships where most everyone was Reformed and went to one of several Reformed churches within a few miles of each other.

Instead, I had to do evangelism to maintain the numbers at my little church (we were always losing people to backsliding or moving out of the neighborhood), and that meant daily interaction with people who weren't Reformed and hadn't grown up Reformed. In that same neighborhood, there were about a half-dozen tiny, struggling Protestant churches. There was a charismatic house church about four blocks from mine; a different, more liberal Dutch Calvinist church about three blocks away; an independent Baptist church on the hill overlooking the neighborhood; a Hispanic fellowship in the government housing project; and others — not to mention churches from the suburbs that would send in buses to gather people for Sunday worship.

I met a lot of people who had grown up Catholic, Methodist, Baptist, or what have you, and were no longer going to church at all. I was trying to convince them to come to my Reformed church, but at some point, they wanted to know what "Reformed" meant and what we believed. So, I was constantly challenged to explain why being "Reformed" was better than Baptist, Methodist, Catholic, or something else. Why should these people start coming to my church, rather than return to the tradition they were raised in? I didn't always have convincing answers.

In trying to evangelize our neighborhood, many of us pastors realized we should not be competing, but that we should try to work together to present a united front of Christian faith to the community. However, whenever we sponsored joint activities, such as a neighborhood "Gospel Fest," it became apparent that our cooperation could not extend very far or very deep. There were too many differences of opinion among us on matters related to the faith, often on important and central issues. We often came to a total impasse when we began to discuss doctrine. They would have their proof texts from Scripture, and I had mine. We would quote our different proof texts, and then talk past one another. After several experiences like this, I began to realize how impossible it was to maintain unity among Christians if all we had to go on was the Bible alone. Everyone, it seemed, had a different *interpretation* of the Bible.

Take baptism, for example. The Dutch Calvinist tradition insisted on infant baptism, and, in fact, regarded it as a sin of negligence not to have one's children baptized. Other groups, like the Baptists and Charismatics, however, regarded infant baptism as a serious mistake, and would only baptize adults, or at least teens above a certain age.

Then there was sexual morality, marriage, and divorce. My church taught the permanence of marriage and that divorce was a sin contrary to Jesus' teaching, as was masturbation. The other, more liberal Dutch Calvinist church had no problem with divorce, if it was part of one's journey of personal development and "finding oneself." Nor was masturbation or other forms of extramarital sex a problem for them. I think they drew the line finally at adultery, but I'm not sure. As for the other churches, there was a wide variety of views and practical applications on questions of sexuality and marriage. The Charismatic group was against extramarital sex in theory, but they never preached on it or confronted anyone about it. The Pentecostal group that sent a bus into the neighborhood was strongly against divorce and encouraged everyone to reconcile with their first spouse if they had been in a string of relationships. So it went.

This really bothered me, so I went to my pastoral mentor, a very accomplished missionary who now taught at a Bible college down the road from my seminary. Over lunch at a nearby restaurant, I posed a question to him like this: "Look, I'm ministering in this neighborhood, and there are at least a half dozen other Protestant churches competing with me for the same people. Each of us is teaching something different, but based on the same Bible. Is this right? Shouldn't we be united?"

My pastoral mentor paused for a moment, and then launched into a historical explanation. "Well, you know, these different groups began to split off from each other starting from the Reformation. You have the Lutherans, first of all, and then the Reformed parted ways from them."

"Wait," I said, "let's hold on right there. I know all the *history*. I've taken all the church history courses at the seminary. What I'm asking is not the historical question of how we got here. What I am asking is a *theological* question: Did Jesus really intend all this diversity of denominations?" My mentor looked at me and paused for a moment, then said slowly, "Well, I guess we'd have to say he did."

I stared back in silence, but inside something popped. "No, he didn't," went silently through my mind. "The same Jesus who prayed 'May they all be one, even as I and the Father are one,' could not possibly have intended forty thousand or more different denominations with different teachings on salvation." That's what I thought, but I didn't say anything, because he was my mentor.

My pastoral mentor continued, trying to explain that all the different denominations were like the colors of the spectrum when white light hits a prism. I thought to myself, "That might work for worship styles. Maybe one church uses a praise band and another an organ. Those cultural tastes can be different from church to church. But differences in doctrine and morality? Jesus cannot have intended that some Christians run around telling people they *must* speak in tongues while others say they *must not*; others claiming we *must* baptize our children while others claim we *must not*; some claiming divorce and remarriage are okay, while others say they are not." Again, that's what I thought, but I didn't say anything, because he was my mentor.

So, as I left that lunch appointment pretty dissatisfied, a new line of thought began to take over my mind.

> "The other pastors I talk to seem pretty obstinate in their views and their scriptural proof-texts. But to them, *I* must seem obstinate. Who's really right? Are they wrong to be non-Reformed, or am I wrong to be Reformed? What right does my Reformed denomination have to exist, anyway? Maybe, for the sake of the unity of Christ's one Church, we should merge with another existing denomination."

This thought bothered me. What right did we have to exist? Was it just obvious that Reformed interpretations of Scripture were right (and everyone else's were wrong)? Was everyone else being deliberately blind to the truth, or were *we* the ones who were out of the loop? I decided to write to one of my favorite and most admired professors, a man known for his erudition, zeal for the Gospel, and commitment to Reformed theology. I posed the question above, basically: "What right does our denomination have to exist?"

He wrote back to me and acknowledged that it was an issue, but that he felt there were certain strong points that our denomination had to offer, which justified our continued existence: like our commitment to Christian education. Well, it's true that my denomination had a big investment in Christian day schools — but then, so did many other denominations. "Heck," I thought, "even the Catholics are into education, and they do it bigger than anyone!" Catholic schools were everywhere, and even Catholic *universities*. By contrast, there was no full-fledged Reformed university in North America, just a half dozen good undergraduate colleges.

It seemed to me that most Christian denominations had a commitment to Christian education to some degree, and many of them were deeply involved. There were Baptist schools, Methodist schools, Lutheran schools, Catholic schools, even Pentecostal schools. With respect, it didn't seem to justify separating the Body of Christ, just to maintain another Christian school system.

So, two of the most respected spiritual men in my life had been unable to answer my questions, questions that originated from the impossibility of coming to agreement among Christians over the meaning of the Scriptures. But there was one more man I wanted to consult. There was a famous theologian in town who had once been a great churchman during my parents' generation. My mother revered him and spoke of what a wise man he had been when he had edited the denominational magazine. Though retired, he was still living, and an older friend of mine knew him quite well. This old theologian had taken to "holding court" in his home. On Saturday mornings, he would welcome area pastors, seminarians, and theological hobbyists over to his house for coffee and theological debate. It wasn't really debate, however, as it mostly consisted of the guests posing questions to the revered theologian and listening to his monologue.

I was eager to go visit this revered theologian and pose my questions to him. So, I begged my older friend to take me along for a Saturday morning "court session," which he was only too eager to do. We arrived one Saturday morning to find four or five pastors and other theological types already gathered around, with the discussion in heated progress. We found chairs and sat down to pick up the thread of conversation. The topic turned out to be church attendance, as well as the fact that the revered theologian had quit going to church, except at the insistence of his wife. In fact, he no longer belonged to any local congregation or denomination. The other participants were perturbed at this development and tried to persuade him, by various arguments, that attending church and loyalty to a denominational organization were important parts of the Christian life. He rejected all these arguments and, being more knowledgeable than all present, could not be persuaded otherwise. At one point he pontificated, "I don't need to belong anywhere. I just want to be a universal Christian, like Billy Graham or the Pope."[1]

Well, that comment rankled me. First of all, there was the hubris to put himself on par with two of the greatest leaders of

---

1   The Pope at this time was Saint John Paul II.

world Christianity. Second, the analogy didn't work. Billy Graham and John Paul II were not independent, "universal" Christians: I was pretty sure Billy Graham was a loyal Southern Baptist, and John Paul II had a very clear loyalty to a certain "denomination." He was Roman Catholic!

At this, my good opinion of the revered theologian started to fade, and the more he talked, the more irritated I got. His reasons for not bothering to go to church were sometimes similar to ones given by the nonpracticing Christians and new converts I worked with on a regular basis. Furthermore, it became clear after a while that he really didn't regard himself as being accountable to anyone else, nor under anyone's authority or pastoral care. He wasn't following Hebrews 13:17.

A kind of youthful, self-righteous indignation filled me up, till I burst out with what I thought was a sound theological rebuke: "You know what your problem is?" I intervened into the theologian's monologue, "You have set yourself up as your own arbiter of the truth!" The revered theologian looked up at me with a bemused expression, as if just noticing that I was there. "Yes, well," he said, without pause or missing a beat, "that is the *Protestant principle*, isn't it?"

My jaw hit the floor, and I dropped back in my chair. The theologian continued lecturing with the other participants, but I had lost interest in the proceedings. I motioned to my friend, who was also tired of the whole discussion, and we excused ourselves. The way home in the car was largely silent. "That is the Protestant principle," kept going through my mind, "Your own arbiter of the truth."

The revered theologian was less pious and devout than I was. But he was more clever and more wise. He had realized the essential nature of Protestantism long before I was willing to admit it to myself. *Sola scriptura* meant that everyone was his own pope. True, the Scripture was above everything … but everyone was left to himself to decide what the Scripture meant.

The third man I admired had let me down. At this point, I was largely done with *sola scriptura*. It led to factions among Christians that could never be resolved. It produced thousands of denominations with no serious reason to exist. It led to a form of maverick Christianity, a kind of religious relativism and subjectivism in which each individual believer decided what was true.

While all this was going on, I was working on a master's thesis for my seminary degree, and my advisor had suggested I write a critique of a recent Old Testament theology from a liberal Protestant theologian. This theologian used a lot of traditional theological language, but in the end his only real commitments seemed to be to the social vision and policies of a particular political party — especially on issues of sexual morality. Rather than upholding and defending what the Scriptures taught and what the Christian tradition had practiced, he endorsed whatever views were popular in society, moving along with the left wing of American culture. For him anything consensual, within or without marriage, was deemed acceptable.

In the process of writing a critique of the very long theology of the Old Testament this theologian had written, I found myself arguing against his scriptural interpretations at every turn. However, in the end it usually ended up as "my word against his." I had my scriptural arguments, and he had his (in my view, twisted) scriptural arguments. To what could I appeal to demonstrate that my position was preferable?

It was at this point in my theological development that I discovered the idea of Christian tradition. Tradition could be our guide! Tradition could arbitrate between competing interpretations of Scripture! In my critique of this theologian's book, I began to appeal again and again to the Christian tradition. We both had our arguments; but mine were in keeping with what Christians had always believed, whereas his were novel, just recent inventions.

Yes, I know. Some of you are saying, "How impressive! Reinventing the wheel, are we?" True enough. I *was* reinventing the wheel. Much later I would learn that the early Fathers already appealed to Tradition to differentiate true Christianity from that of the heretics. But I was new to this. Although I was completing my seminary career, I was nothing more than a baby theologian, a theological infant, a neophyte. There was so much I did not know, because no one bothered to expose me to it, or at least to point out its significance and implications.

Our Lady's University

The problem of *sola scriptura*, the intractable differences of interpretation among Protestants, the problem of being one's own arbiter of truth, and all these other issues kept swirling in my head, yet the time was coming to receive ordination and commit to a career in my denomination. But I didn't even have a clear idea of why my denomination needed to exist! This was a real crisis for me. I had prepared for almost ten years of undergraduate and graduate education to be a pastor; and now I stood at the threshold and didn't know if I should commit.

I felt discouraged, disillusioned, and directionless. We could throw in some other D's as well: despondent and disoriented. I didn't know what to do with my life, and I had a wife and three children to support. So, I did something drastic that many in a similar situation of despair and disorientation have also done: I applied to graduate school.

I figured that doing a doctorate in biblical studies would give me something profitable to do for a few years while I sorted out my head and tried to align with the right Christian group, one that I could really believe in, not simply one I was born into. With that in mind, I applied to a dozen graduate schools for a doctorate in Scripture and got accepted by the University of Notre Dame.

I've already mentioned how I met Michael there, and how he was able to give a scriptural defense of some Catholic doctrines I thought were indefensible. One day as we were discussing theology, he posed a question to me: "Where in Scripture does it teach *sola scriptura*?" he asked innocently.

That question took me aback. I had never been asked that before. *Sola scriptura* was something we *assumed* as Protestants. I didn't know the scriptural basis for it.

The first verse that came to my mind is the one that occurs to most Protestants: "Well," I said to Michael, "There is that verse in one of Paul's letters to Timothy." I grabbed a Bible and started to look, because I could never remember the exact reference. But I found it quickly enough. It was 2 Timothy 3:16:

> All Scripture is inspired by God and profitable for teaching, for reproof, for correction, and for training in righteousness.

I read the verse to Michael, but he and I could both see it didn't really teach *sola scriptura*. Any Catholic could also agree that "all Scripture is inspired by God and is profitable" for many things. It's just not sufficient by itself for the whole of the Christian life.

Now, some Protestants push this verse as a proof-text for *sola scriptura* by pressing the meaning of word translated above as "profitable." In Greek, the word is *ophelimos*, "helpful," but some Protestant apologists stretch the meaning into "sufficient," giving the following translation:

> All Scripture is inspired by God and *sufficient* for teaching, for reproof, for correction, and for training in righteousness.

"See!" they say, "Scripture is sufficient for everything we need!" The problem is, *ophelimos* does not mean "sufficient." It simply means "helpful."

"You know," Michael said, "there really isn't any passage of Scripture that teaches *sola scriptura*."

"Hmmph," I snorted in reluctant assent, because I couldn't think of any, either.

"But there is a verse that Catholics like to point to that explains the need for both written Scriptures and oral tradition. Second Thessalonians 2:15." I looked it up in my Bible, which was the New International Version. It read as follows:

> So then, brothers and sisters, stand firm and hold fast to the teachings we passed on to you, whether by word of mouth or by letter.

"You see," Michael explained, "the teachings passed down by letter are the New Testament epistles, in other words, Scripture. But Saint Paul also stresses being faithful to teachings by 'word of mouth,' in other words, oral tradition. The meaning would be clearer if you weren't reading from a Protestant translation."

It was here that I learned something unusual about certain Protestant translations of the Bible, at least the one I used, the New International Version (NIV). The Greek language has a word, *paradosis*, that means "tradition." The NIV, in fact, translates this word as "tradition" most of the times it occurs in the New Testament — *whenever it has a negative connotation*, like when Jesus criticizes the tradition of the Pharisees.[2]

However, three times in the New Testament the word *paradosis* has a very positive connotation, because it refers to Christian tradition rather than Pharisaic. In those three instances, however, the New International Version translates *paradosis* as "teaching" rather than "tradition." The effect of this, however, is to form Christian readers who think that the New Testament never has anything positive to say about tradition! But that just isn't the case. The following verses are very important, and reflect the crucial role that tradition began to play even within the lifetime of Saint Paul:

> I commend you because you remember me in everything and maintain the traditions [*paradoseis*] even as I have delivered them to you. (1 Cor 11:2)

> So then, brethren, stand firm and hold to the traditions [*paradoseis*] which you were taught by us, either by word of mouth or by letter. (2 Thess 2:15)

> Now we command you, brethren, in the name of our Lord Jesus Christ, that you keep away from any brother who is living in idleness and not in accord with the tradition [*paradosin*] that you received from us. (2 Thess 3:6)

Though these are only three verses, I can't stress how distorting it is to grow up without these testimonies to the good function of tradition. This contributed to my youthful, zealous attitude that rejected even the Reformed tradition in my early seminary days. To me at that time, being Reformed meant opposing any and all tradition, because I associated it with the Pharisees and Catholics.

---

2   Matt 15:3, 6; Mark 7:3–5, 8–9, 13; Col 2:8.

If anyone wishes to say, "But there are only three verses that stress tradition as good!" let me remind readers that there are only two verses in the New Testament that use the phrase "born again" (John 3:3, 7)! In both cases, the phrase is probably better translated either "born anew" or "born from above"! Despite that, many people characterize themselves as "born again" Christians. The Bible says less about being "born again" than it does about holding fast to tradition. So, ironically, there is no verse or passage of the New or Old Testaments that teaches "the Bible alone," but there are three that stress the importance of holding on to tradition, and one that distinguishes two kinds of tradition: oral and written (2 Thess 2:15).

During the early years after I became a Catholic, when old friends were still contacting me and wanted to talk me out of my Catholicism, I found an easy way to end the debate (if I was tired and didn't want to argue) was just to say, "Okay, fine: show me where the Bible teaches *sola scriptura.*" It would always be the same thing. First, 2 Tim 3:16, then discovering that *ophelimos* doesn't mean what Protestants need it to mean. Then, various other even less plausible arguments: the warnings against adding anything to the sacred book that occur at the end of Revelation (22:18–19) and in passages of Deuteronomy (4:2, 12:32). But these only apply to those two books, not to the Bible as a whole. Besides, neither teaches that Scripture alone is sufficient for the Christian life and the health of the Church. Finally, there are vague appeals to the "implications" or "assumptions" that are "obvious" in the teaching of Jesus and the apostles, to the effect that Scripture is sufficient. But the implications and assumptions are clearly not obvious, because in three places the New Testament, as we have seen, stresses the importance of tradition in addition to the written Scriptures.

The Scriptures are right to stress this unwritten tradition, because one of the things that was handed on in unwritten form was the proper list of inspired biblical books themselves! The "table of contents" of the Old and New Testaments were never written down by an inspired author. Early Church councils at the end of the A.D. 300s drew up the "table of contents" that we call the "list of canonical books."[3] They drew the list from oral tradition and from the practice and customs of Christian worship, which preserved the tradition handed down from the apostles concerning which books were canonical and which weren't. Ironically, then, the "table of contents" of the written Scriptures actually comes from *unwritten tradition*. Therefore, you can't attack the value of unwritten tradition without, finally, undermining Scripture itself.

In fact, not only does Scripture testify to the importance of tradition, it also explicitly teaches what to do when there is a problem of interpretation. This is a truth that I failed to realize until years of being a Catholic. As Protestants, we would talk about the Bible as being "perspicuous" (that is, clear) on all important subjects, and "self-interpreting." The Bible did not need interpretation, because it interpreted itself! I had a pastor tell me once: "It is the devil who makes you think the Bible needs to be interpreted." He advocated the view that all you needed to do was read difficult passages in light of clearer ones, and apply a few other rules, and *voila!* — you had instant meaning from any passage you wanted.

Of course, that's a naïve approach that is only convincing when one is young, passionate, and unfamiliar with the real difficulty of interpreting all the thousands of passages that make up the two Testaments. In reality, the Old Testament gives instructions for what to do when you cannot interpret God's word in a given situation:

> If there arise a matter too hard for you in judgment, between blood and blood, between plea and plea, and between stroke and stroke, being matters of controversy within your gates: then you shall arise, and go up to the place which the LORD your God shall choose; And you shall come to the priests the Levites, and to the judge that shall be in those days, and inquire; and they shall show you the sentence of judgment: And you shall do according to

---

3 The Councils of Rome (382), Hippo (393), Carthage (419), and Florence (1441-42) affirmed the Catholic canon of Scripture, as did Augustine, Aquinas, Bonaventure, and other Church Fathers and Doctors.

the sentence, which they of that place which the LORD shall choose shall show you; and you shall observe to do according to all that they inform you: According to the sentence of the law which they shall teach you, and according to the judgment which they shall tell you, you shall do: you shall not decline from the sentence which they shall show you, to the right hand, nor to the left. And the man that will do presumptuously, and will not listen to the priest that stands to minister there before the LORD your God, or to the judge — that man shall die: and you shall put away the evil from Israel. (Deut 17:8–12)[4]

What is at stake here is the interpretation of God's Word. In practice, the most important part of God's word to the children of Israel was the laws that governed their daily life. Should some situation arise in which different laws seemed to conflict, and it was difficult to adjudicate, the ancient Israelites could have recourse to the central sanctuary — which was first the Tabernacle and later the Temple — and there seek a judgment from the Levitical priests and/or the civil judge, or the two of them together — probably representing canon law and civil law respectively.

This means that Deuteronomy, the last and greatest statement of the Mosaic Covenant, did not consider itself a *self-interpreting or perspicuous document*. This pivotal and climactic book of the Old Covenant provided for a way to interpret itself, but this way presumed a living, identifiable community with living, identifiable priest-judges who could authoritatively adjudicate for the whole people. Each individual Israelite was not tasked with the responsibility of interpreting divine law on his own.

Likewise, a similar situation holds in the New Covenant. Jesus does not leave it up to each individual follower to interpret Jesus' teachings for himself. Instead, as we have seen, Jesus bestows authority on Peter (Matt 16:18–19) and upon the apostles as a group (Matt 18:18) to "bind and loose" for the New Covenant people of God, that is to say, to authoritatively interpret divine law

---

4 I have employed the King James Version here, because it is the most literal, but I have modernized the grammatical forms and pronouns.

for the community. Already in chapter five, on the priesthood, we have seen how this authority was shared with others in the lifetime of the apostles themselves, and a transmission or succession of authority was set up, to which the earliest of the Fathers also testify. So, the author of Hebrews can say, "Obey your leaders and submit to their authority" confident that the Christians to whom he wrote actually did have leaders who were already in authority. This is the point: the New Testament *presupposes that the Church already exists.* The New Testament doesn't give any instructions on setting up a church, because it's already been set up, by Jesus on the shoulders of the apostles, who handed on leadership to others.

Neither the Old Testament nor the New Testament is self-interpreting. Both Testaments anticipated that there would be controversy over interpretation, and both made clear who had the authority to adjudicate controversy. In the Old Testament, it was the Levitical priests and the judge who worked at the central sanctuary of the nation. In the New Testament, it is Peter and the apostles as a group, whose authority has passed to their successors.

Ultimately, the testimony of Scripture is *against sola scriptura.* Ironically, the Scriptures themselves make provision for the adjudication of disputes about Scripture, but the provision they provide appeals to a living community with leaders who already exist, who can be found and located. Both Testaments presume the existence of the People of God as a visible community with visible office bearers. The interpretation of the Scriptures only becomes an unsolvable, factious dilemma when Christians reject the visible church and its visible office bearers, and seek to set up different churches according to their own concepts or convictions.

CHAPTER SEVEN

Losing Faith in "Faith Alone"

Sola fide, or "faith alone," was the other Protestant concept that toppled for me during my years of ministry. The idea of *sola fide*, however, can sound noble and appealing, and can be presented that way: "God loves us so much and he knows we are so weak, so he doesn't require anything of us except that we trust him. If we trust him, he is so merciful he will forgive all the sins we continue to do and take us to himself because of the atoning sacrifice of Jesus Christ alone. Anyone who says works are necessary for salvation is just a Pharisee and a legalist who wants to burden people with obligations, obscuring the free gift of God that is salvation through faith alone." I understand the appeal of this way of thinking and speaking, and certain parts of it are true. However, in the end it is a subtle but significant misunderstanding of the Gospel preached by Jesus and the apostles.

In the practice of urban ministry, I found that preaching "salvation by faith alone" was generally understood to mean salvation by belief in certain facts about Jesus: his divinity, his resurrection, his desire to forgive, and so on. Provided these facts were believed, one would be saved — regardless of one's subsequent behavior.

I was trained to evangelize by going door to door and telling people that they were saved by faith in Jesus Christ alone, and that their works, behavior, or choices had no role at all in their salvation. A rather dramatic incident illustrates this.

My pastoral mentor, a plain-spoken, heavy-set former cop who had felt a call to urban ministry, would take me on follow-up visits to neighborhood residents who had visited one of our worship services. On one call, a middle-aged woman invited us up to her dilapidated second-floor apartment, where we shared the basic outline of the Gospel with her, and she prayed the "sinners' prayer": a prayer asking to receive Jesus into her life.

That was a wonderful moment, and both my mentor and I were elated. What followed, however, was not so edifying. My urban pastor friend began to catechize the woman by asking her, "So, now that you have prayed to receive Jesus, if you went out tomorrow and shot someone, would you still be saved?"

A confused look came over the woman's face, and she just managed, "Uhhh...."

But my mentor pressed further, "Yes, and if next week, say, you robbed a bank and left town in a stolen car, would you still be saved?"

"Uhhh.... No?" the woman guessed.

"Yes, you would!" my pastor friend exclaimed triumphantly. "Because once saved, always saved! Now that you've put your faith in Jesus, you can never lose your salvation, because salvation is based on your faith, and not on anything you do!"

I sat back watching this whole interaction unfold, a bit shocked by the direction my mentor had chosen to pursue. I found myself thinking, "Wait. I agree with the woman. If you just profess faith in Jesus but continue to commit crimes, that's a pretty good indication that you are not truly saved."

A whole slew of Scripture verses started coming to my mind:

> "If anyone would come after me, he must deny himself, take up his cross daily, and follow me." (Luke 9:23)

> "Not everyone who says to me, 'Lord, Lord!' will be saved, but only he who does the will of my father in heaven." (Matt 7:21)

> What does it profit, my brothers, if a man says he has faith but has not works? (James 2:14)

It's true that I paid lip service to the concept of *sola fide*, or faith alone. However, I believed that true faith *necessarily* brought forth good works. If you had no good works, you did not have true faith. Nevertheless, I had continued to deny that the *works* played any actual role in one's salvation.

I had never seen the concept of "faith alone" carried to such an extreme as my pastoral mentor did, even telling new converts that serious sins did not endanger their salvation. I knew in my heart that this was wrong, because it was never the way that Jesus himself presented the Gospel. Jesus was up front about the demands of following him. *"The gate is narrow and the way is hard, that leads to life, and those who find it are few"* (Matt 7:14).

In time, as I dealt with many people in the inner city, I often encountered this extreme view of "faith alone" advocated by my older friend. This was brought home to me through a painful pastoral experience. A woman in our congregation, a single mom and faithful churchgoer, moved in with her boyfriend with the full knowledge of the congregation. All of us lived within a few blocks of the church, so there were few — if any — secrets in the community. This was a cause of scandal, especially because we were expending great efforts to encourage the teens of the church to remain chaste before marriage. I made repeated pastoral visits to this dear woman, reminding her of her Christian commitment, and reviewing with her the texts of Scripture that warned against sexual behavior outside of marriage. Yet the situation did not change. Finally, I asked her to meet with myself and the other elders of the congregation, and to my surprise, she did. Gently, and as her spiritual brothers, we encouraged her to break off the relationship or else marry her boyfriend. She listened to all this with admirable patience, but when we had finished all we had to say, her final response was: "I know that what I am doing is wrong. But I also know I'm saved by faith, not by works. I still believe. So, I know I'm going to heaven, and I'm not going to move out."

That was a jaw-dropping experience for me, because I had not often in my life witnessed people making a clear, conscious decision to do something they knew and openly admitted was against the will of God. It remains one of only a half-dozen or less such blatant occasions I have seen firsthand before or since. It occurred to me that this woman had been converted under my pastoral mentor, who advocated that extreme form of salvation by faith alone.

Although I could qualify what *sola fide* meant in such a way as to affirm it formally and theoretically, in practice I switched my methods of evangelism and catechesis to emphasize the indwelling of Christ, whose presence grants both eternal life and holiness. My touchstone passages became those of 1 John, such as "He who has the son, has life. He who has not the Son of God has not life" (1 John 5:12) and "We know that anyone born of God does not sin" (5:18).

A More Responsible View of "Salvation by Faith Alone"

To be fair, most of the Protestant pastors I knew had a much more balanced view of this doctrine. They would emphasize that, although salvation was by "faith alone," nonetheless, *true faith* or *saving faith* necessarily resulted in good works. If you didn't see the fruit of good works in your life, it meant you didn't have true faith. Viewed this way, good works were very important, because if you didn't have them, it meant you hadn't converted and were going to hell. This way of viewing "salvation by faith alone" leads to scrupulosity in some streams of the Calvinist tradition. While many Protestants understood "salvation by faith alone" to mean they just had to believe and nothing else was necessary, some groups within the Reformed or Calvinist tradition saw good works as a very important sign of one's salvation, and therefore ended up sometimes being a bit morally rigorous or even legalistic. It's interesting that the same theoretical doctrine can be interpreted in different ways and lead to very different forms of piety.

The more balanced view, that true faith produces good works, is what I taught while catechizing new Christians in the first years of my work in urban ministry. After a while, I picked up a copy of the *Catechism of the Catholic Church* that, ironically, had been given to me by the same pastor who trained me in evangelization. Even more strange, he had fished several of them out of a bin of damaged books from a local *Calvinist* publishing house (!) that had subcontracted to print the *Catechism of the Catholic Church* in the United States (!). Yes, life is that strange.

In any event, I started perusing the *Catechism* and realized that its treatment of faith, works, and justification was not the caricature of "earning one's way to heaven" by "getting gold stars for attending sacraments" that I had been told by cynical Protestant pastors. In fact, its treatment was pretty balanced, giving primary emphasis to faith and God's grace, which enables us to live lives pleasing to God. I had the distinct feeling that, by the time one had made all the qualifications necessary to "salvation by faith alone" to avoid the caricature view that one just believed and then could go on a murderous rampage without fear of losing salvation, one would have walked himself backward into the Catholic view of salvation via the kitchen door. If responsible Catholics and Protestants ended up basically in the same place — faith is primary, but works are necessary — I began to wonder what value there was in maintaining lip service to this slogan "salvation by faith alone," especially since "faith alone" only appears in the New Testament when James is dismissing it (James 2:24). It just seemed to provide an opportunity for misunderstanding.

Faith Alone and Jesus' Preaching

Preaching, catechizing, evangelizing and my own meditation kept me in contact with the Gospels, and I noticed how Jesus' methods of evangelism were not like the training I received. Jesus did not preach "salvation by faith alone" the way folks usually understood that phrase.

Indeed, in hindsight, it amazes me how this emphasis on salvation by faith apart from works is so contrary to the preaching of Jesus in the Gospels. One can take any Gospel, start reading, and find passage after passage in which Jesus teaches things that contradict the whole *sola fide* mind-set. Let's just proceed a little way into the Gospel of Matthew, for example.

Jesus begins his preaching by proclaiming, "Repent! For the kingdom of heaven is at hand!" (Matt 4:17). "Repentance" involves feeling sorrow for sin, and turning away from sin. One does not repent by continuing to indulge in sin.

Jesus then calls his first disciples, telling them to "follow me" (4:18–22). In ancient Jewish culture, following a rabbi meant imitating him in absolutely everything he did, down to the way he ate and how he interacted with his wife (if the rabbi were married). This command to "follow me" would involve a complete transformation of the lives of these fishermen, not merely a change of belief.

Jesus then goes up a mountain top, and proceeds to preach the Sermon on the Mount. He begins by pronouncing blessings on people who exhibit certain *behaviors* and *dispositions*: poverty of spirit, sorrow for sin, meekness, purity of heart, mercifulness, desire for righteousness, and so on. Then he uses "salt" and "light" as metaphors for the "good works" that his disciples should perform in order that others will see and give glory to God (5:16). None of the commandments of the Law will be relaxed (v. 19), and "unless your righteousness exceeds that of the scribes and Pharisees, you will never enter the kingdom of heaven." Does any of this sound like "faith alone"?

The body of the Sermon on the Mount consists of *practical* instructions on how to live: how to handle anger (5:21–26), sexual desire (5:27–30), marital commitment (5:31–32), oath swearing (5:33–37), insults (5:38–42), enemies (5:43–48), almsgiving (6:1–4), prayer (6:5–15), and fasting (6:16–17). Why all this practical instruction if our works don't contribute to our salvation?

Skipping to the end of the Sermon on the Mount, Jesus seems to teach directly against some contemporary understandings of "salvation by faith alone":

> "Not everyone who says to me, 'Lord, Lord,' shall enter the kingdom of heaven, but *he who does the will of my Father who is in heaven!*" (Matt 7:21, emphasis added)

How much more clarity can we ask for? Our Lord is explicitly saying, "Talk is cheap. It's those who *practice* my teachings who will enter the kingdom!"

Again, the final parable of the Sermon on the Mount contrasts the wise man who "hears these words of mine *and does them,*" versus the foolish man who "hears these words of mine and *does not do them.*" The wise man builds his house on rock, but as for the fool — well, as many of us learned from a famous

Sunday School rhyme, the "the rains came down and the floods came up … and the house came a-tumblin' down!" The contrast between the wise and foolish man is not between belief and unbelief, but between *doing* and *not doing*!

So it goes through the whole Gospel of Matthew, and the other Gospels as well. We don't have time to review them all, but suffice it to say, the doctrine of "salvation by faith alone" was not derived from the Gospels. I realized this just from reading and teaching the Bible as an inner-city pastor. To be sure, *belief* in Jesus is important, but the person who truly *believes* Jesus will also obey his commandments. It's part of a package deal.

No, "salvation by faith alone" was not derived from the Gospels. It was derived from the Epistle to the Romans, as many of us know from popular biographies of Martin Luther. This best-known of the Protestant Reformers formed his ideas on faith and salvation while reading Saint Paul's longest and perhaps most important letter. However, Romans does not teach "salvation by faith alone" in the sense that phrase is usually understood by contemporary Protestants. In fact, Romans is very Roman Catholic. Its teaching on salvation is entirely consistent with what the Catholic Church has always taught about how we are saved. So, now I would like to examine Romans more closely.

Roman Theology in the Letter to the Romans

Paul's Letter to the Romans is perhaps his most thorough doctrinal statement, and it begins and ends with the phrase "obedience of faith" (1:5, 16:27). In fact, one could argue that "obedience of faith" is the theme of the letter.

Contemporary Protestants and Catholics tend to understand "obedience of faith" in two different ways. For many Protestants, "obedience of faith" means "an obedience that consists simply in faith." That means, the only obedience God requires is to believe. For the Catholic Church, however, "the obedience of faith" means "a true obedience that is empowered and enabled by faith." In other words, faith in Jesus makes it possible for you to obey God.

That's because Protestants and Catholics conceive of salvation in different ways; one as a *juridical* event, the other as an *ontological* event.[1] For classic Protestantism, salvation is like a courtroom acquittal: God the Father slams down the gavel and declares you free to go, because Jesus suffered your sentence for you. For Catholics, the analogy is not like a courtroom, but more like a scene from a superhero movie. You are the scrawny and sickly sinner, but you enter the power-up chamber (i.e., the sacraments) and emerge as Captain America! That is, placing one's faith in Jesus and receiving the sacraments imparts to you the Holy Spirit, which actually *changes* your *nature*, not just your *legal* status before God.

Which vision is more in keeping with Paul's teaching in Romans? Well, let's move briefly through this epistle and try to look with fresh eyes at what Saint Paul actually teaches.

Paul states the thesis of his epistle in Romans 1:16–17 ("the good news is the power of salvation for everyone with faith") and then begins to share the "bad news" for which the "good news" is the cure. This "bad news" is the sinfulness of mankind, which Paul describes in Rom 1:18–32.

In the following chapter (Rom 2), Paul warns about the wrath of God that is coming because of this sinfulness. In this very chapter, Paul repeatedly emphasizes that there is a coming judgment on mankind that will be based on humanity's *actions* and *behavior*, not merely on wrong *belief*. I can't quote the whole chapter (you can read it yourself), but I will mention some excerpts to convey the force of Paul's point:

> For He [God] will render *to every man according to his works*: to those who by patience in well-doing seek for glory … he will give eternal life; but for those who … obey wickedness, there will be wrath…. (Rom 2:6–9, emphasis added)

> There will be tribulation and distress for every human being who *does evil,* … but glory … for every one who *does good.*… (Rom 2:9–10, emphasis added)

---

1 "Juridical" means "having to do with the law," whereas "ontological" means "having to do with being or essence."

> For it is not the hearers of the law who are righteous be-
> fore God, but *the doers of the law who will be justified*.
> (Rom 2:13, emphsis added)

It is truly amazing that in the very book of the Bible many imagine teaches "faith alone" most clearly, Paul outright says that everyone will be judged according to works, and the doing of the
law leads to justification!

Of course, many will think, "What then of those texts in
Romans that *do* seem to teach a 'faith alone' perspective? How
can we understand them?" In the next chapter of Romans (chapter 3), Saint Paul makes statements that many have taken in a
wrong direction:

> For no human being will be justified in his sight by *works
> of the law*, since through the law comes knowledge of sin.
> (Rom 3:20, emphasis added)

> For we hold that a man is justified by faith apart from
> *works of law*. (Rom 3:28, emphasis added)

This latter verse (3:28) is probably the closest Paul ever comes to
saying that we are saved by faith alone. But what he specifically
says is that we are justified by faith *apart from works of the law*.
The key to understanding this verse is the meaning of the phrase
"works of the law."

To modern ears, it sounds like "works in keeping with the
moral law," that is, good works. But that is not what "works of the
law" meant in the Judaism of Saint Paul's day!

Let me explain. The only other body of literature from the
time of Saint Paul that uses the phrase "works of the law" is the
Dead Sea Scrolls. From them, we learn that "works of the law"
was a technical term referring to ceremonial practices of ritual
cleanliness of the Old Covenant.

For example, among the Dead Sea Scrolls we find several
copies of a letter that was written by the leaders of the Dead Sea
religious community (called "Qumran") to the Pharisees who
were in control of religious practice in Jerusalem at the time.

The Essene[2] leaders of Qumran write to correct the Pharisees on twenty-two different issues of cultic purity, including things like how to handle leather, dogs in Jerusalem, streams of liquid from one vessel to another, Gentile-grown wheat, lepers, human bones, and priestly marriages. The Essenes believed that the Pharisees meant well, but did not understand how properly to interpret the Mosaic Law governing these issues — in other words, they were "binding and loosing" incorrectly. At the conclusion of their letter, the Essenes wrote the following:

> And also we have written to you some of *the works of the Law* which we think are good for you and for your people, for we s[a]w that you have intellect and knowledge of the Law. Reflect on all these matters and seek from him that he may support your counsel and keep far from you the evil scheming{s} and the counsel of Belial, so that at the end of time, you may rejoice in finding that some of our words are true. And *it shall be reckoned to you as righteous* when you do what is upright and good before him, for your good and that of Israel.[3]

We can see immediately that this conclusion of the letter uses two phrases that are very important in Paul's letters: "works of the law" (see Rom. 3:20; Gal. 2:16, 3:2, 5, 10) and "reckoned as justice/righteousness" (see Rom 4:3–5, 9–11, 22; Gal 3:6; James 2:23).

But what is the context? What does "works of the law" mean here? Well, the Essenes say they have written to the Pharisees about "some of the works of the law." What was it they wrote about? Giving food to the hungry? Clothing the naked? Comforting the sorrowful? No! They wrote about nothing that would come under the category of good works or works of charity. They wrote about ritual handling of leather, dogs, bones, and the such

---

2 The Essenes were a holiness sect of ancient Judaism, the third largest Jewish sect after the Pharisees and Sadducees.

3 F. García Martínez and E. J. C. Tigchelaar, *The Dead Sea Scrolls Study Edition, Vol. 2* (Leiden; New York: Brill, 1997–1999), 803; slightly adapted by myself to be better understood by English-speaking Christian readers.

like. These are matters that have traditionally been called the "ceremonial precepts of the Old Covenant" in Christian theology.

So, based on how the phrase is used in the Jewish literature contemporary with Saint Paul (i.e., the Scrolls), the "works of the law" in Paul should be understood as referring to the ceremonies of the Mosaic Law, things like circumcision, keeping kosher, ritual washings, and the like. Returning to the key verse of Romans 3:28:

> For we hold that a man is justified by faith apart from *works of law.*

Paul's primary meaning here is not that good works are an unnecessary part of the process of salvation, but that it is by faith in Christ that we are changed and made just, not by observing the *external ceremonies of the Old Covenant.*

This is Paul's Gospel in Romans: through faith in Christ we receive the Holy Spirit, and the Holy Spirit "justifies" us, that is, makes us just, makes us able to do what is right and fulfill God's law (the moral law). Observing the "works of the Law" of Moses — circumcision, kosher, and so on — will never transform us the way the Holy Spirit does when we receive Him through faith. Thus, it is through faith that we are made just, apart from the ceremonial works of the law. Once having been made just by the Spirit through faith, however, we must follow the Spirit and live lives of holiness. The Spirit makes a holy life possible, but it does require our cooperation.

All of this becomes clear in the heart of Romans, which is chapter 8, verses 1–17. For the sake of time and space, forgive me for cutting this passage to its essentials:

> (V. 2) The law of the Spirit of life in Christ Jesus has set me free from the law of sin and death … (v. 4) in order that *the just requirement of the law might be fulfilled in us,* who walk not according to the flesh but according to the Spirit…. (v. 13) For *if you live according to the flesh you will die,* but if by the Spirit you put to death the deeds of the body you will live … (v. 16) the Spirit himself bearing witness with our spirit that we are children of God, (v. 17) and if children, then heirs,

142 Losing Faith in "Faith Alone"

heirs of God and fellow heirs with Christ, *provided we suffer with him* in order that we may also be glorified with him.

It is important that all Christians look carefully at what Saint Paul is saying here! Is he saying that we can just believe in Jesus and then go lie, rob, and kill, and still go to heaven? Certainly not! He says that the Holy Spirit enables us to "fulfill the just requirement of the law," a way of referring to the moral law of God, summed up in the twin commands of love of God and neighbor. If we continue to "live according to the flesh" even after receiving the Holy Spirit, we will "die"! This refers to the second death, condemnation to hell! But rather, if we deny our lusts and sinful desires by "putting to death the deeds of the body by the Spirit," then we will "live" eternally! This is not always easy or pleasant to accept, but Saint Paul warns us that if we desire to be "glorified" with Christ, we must "suffer with him."

The teaching of Romans 8 allows us to reconcile some of the seemingly contradictory things that Saint Paul says earlier in Romans. In Romans 2, Saint Paul emphasized that we would be judged by our works: this is true. Those who do evil because they refuse the gift of the Holy Spirit will be condemned, but those who receive the Holy Spirit through faith and thus are enabled to do good works, will be rewarded. In Romans 3, Saint Paul emphasized that we are "justified" by faith and not by "works of the law." This is true, because it is through faith that the Holy Spirit comes into our lives and changes us, enabling and empowering us to do what is right. Following the "works of the law" like circumcision, Sabbath observance, ritual washing, and so on, will never transform us like the Holy Spirit can.

So, then, are we justified by works? No! The Holy Spirit makes us just. Works don't change us. Thereafter, however, we are empowered by the Holy Spirit to do the good works that arise from faith, and thus be able to stand at the judgment before God, being judged by the works that the Spirit enabled us to do. This does, however, involve the cooperation with the Spirit in our lives, and it involves suffering, because the "flesh" — the biblical term for what the Church often calls "concupiscence" or the root of evil desire — remains in us. It is this that must be "put to death" through the power of the Spirit.

This is not the place for an exhaustive commentary on the Epistle to the Romans, and I know there are many other passages that we have not dealt with. Paul says many complex and subtle things in Romans 6 and 7. Furthermore, Saint Paul doesn't make things easy on us, because he uses the term "law" in many different ways in Romans. Sometimes "law" means the Old Testament Scriptures (3:19), or the Pentateuch (3:21), or the natural/moral law (2:14), or the conscience (2:15), or the principle of something (8:2). Sorting it all out is not easy, and that's why so many commentaries are written on Romans.

Nonetheless, I can say with confidence that all that Paul teaches in this letter is compatible with the model of salvation that I have laid out above: faith in Christ grants us the Holy Spirit, who enables us to fulfill the moral law (love of God and neighbor) and thus truly be pleasing to God when we stand before him in judgment. Much more can be said — notably, the forgiveness of sins and the sacraments need to be included in this picture — but this much is true.

Catholics and "Works Righteousness"

So, now that I'm a Catholic, do I think I'm perfect and can earn my way to heaven? Far from it! But I truly believe that I do possess the Holy Spirit, granted to me through faith and the sacraments of baptism (Acts 2:38) and confirmation (Acts 8:17). This Spirit is renewed and enlivened in me through the Eucharist (John 6:56) and confession (James 5:14–16; 1 John 1:9). I know I still sin (1 John 1:8), but also know that I have truly made progress in following Christ, not by any good thing in myself, but only by his grace (Eph 2:8–10).

Becoming Catholic did make a difference in my spiritual life. As a Protestant, I often despaired of making any real progress in the spiritual life, and grew accustomed to habitual sins, not thinking that they would substantively affect my salvation in any way, since it was all by "faith." Of course, since I was cut off from the sacraments of the Eucharist and Reconciliation, it is no wonder that I despaired of progress in the spiritual life. Now, as a Catholic, I know that progress is possible, and that I have the means, provided by God through the body of Christ (the Church), to make that progress. Not only is it possible, but it is necessary, because I must "put to death the deeds of the body by the Spirit" and "suffer" with Christ if I wish to share in his glory.

I return to an insight that I have probably already shared, an insight that came to me only when I was in my forties and had already been Catholic for a long time: Jesus came to save us from our *sins*, not just from the *consequences of our sins* (i.e., hell). To be "saved from our sins" means we really do stop sinning, or at least that there is progress in this area. Sin is not a path to happiness or well-being. Sin is turning away from God, turning away from life toward death. We can't be "saved" and experience life unless we turn toward and embrace God, who is the opposite of sin. I think this whole process of salvation is summed up beautifully by Saint Paul in Romans 5:1–5, with which I will conclude:

> Therefore, since we are justified by faith, we have peace with God through our Lord Jesus Christ. Through him we have obtained access to this grace in which we stand, and we rejoice in our hope of sharing the glory of God. More than that, we rejoice in our sufferings, knowing that suffering produces endurance, and endurance produces character, and character produces hope, and hope does not disappoint us, because God's love has been poured into our hearts through the Holy Spirit which has been given to us. (Rom 5:1–5)